flea market WITHDRAWN chic

flea market *chic*

the thrifty way to create a stylish home

Liz Bauwens and
Alexandra Campbell

Photography by
Simon Brown

CICO BOOKS
LONDON NEW YORK
www.cicobooks.com

Published in 2012 by CICO Books
An imprint of Ryland Peters & Small Ltd
20–21 Jockey's Fields   519 Broadway, 5th Floor
London WC1R 4BW   New York, NY 10012

www.cicobooks.com

10 9 8 7 6 5 4 3 2

For Lois, Milo, and Finn, and for Rosie and Freddie.

A CIP catalog record for this book is available from
the Library of Congress and the British Library.

ISBN 978 1 908170 15 6

Printed in China

Editor: Gillian Haslam
Copy editor: Carmel Edmonds
Designer: Louise Leffler
Photographer: Simon Brown

contents

introduction

The term "flea market" evokes Parisian street-markets and the apparently effortless chic of someone who comes back from shopping with something unusual or beautiful. And they've paid about as much as you did for your coffee and croissant in exactly the same street. How do they do it? Do you have to get up at dawn, or know the vendors? Do you have to spend years learning about a particular era? Is this something that only very artistic people can pull off? Or are flea-market shoppers lying about how much they paid?

Some flea-market shoppers are very knowledgeable or artistic, or they do get up very early, but the real secret to flea-market shopping is enthusiasm and patience. This book will show you how to shop effectively and find great bargains. Go regularly—have a look around your local thrift or charity shop every time you pass by it. Don't expect to find something every time. You won't find inspiring displays and you will see a lot of things you don't like. But look under a table or behind an ugly vase, and you will suddenly spot that magical find.

Flea markets have changed a great deal in recent years. Some of the most famous ones, such as the Sunday market at L'Isle-sur-la-Sorgue in the south of France, now sell mainly new stock. They are exciting and atmospheric (and often sell good-quality craft work), but they're more of a tourist attraction than a flea market. However, the big antique trade fairs, such as the UK's Sunbury Antiques Market at Kempton Park in Surrey, which open at 6am, are closed by lunchtime, and are mainly full of professional dealers, still have a "flea market" feel.

But the true heir to yesterday's flea markets are where secondhand goods are either sold by their owners or donated to charity in a clearout. Every country has slightly different terminology. In the United States and Canada they are more likely to be called "garage sales" or "yard sales," while in the UK, there are "car boot sales". Australians may use the term "swap meet", along with "garage sale." Australia, the US, and Canada describe shops that raise money for charity with donated goods as "thrift stores," while the UK calls them "charity shops". In France, look out for *vides grenier*, *dépôt-ventes*, *marchés aux puces*, and *brocantes*, and in Italy, *soffitte in piazza* literally means "attics in the street." As there are so many different words for these sales all over the world, we have used the word "fair" to cover everything from a yard sale to a car boot fair. And, of course, the online auction website eBay could be considered a huge, international flea market.

What flea markets sell has changed, too. Finds from the 19th and early 20th centuries are now harder to find and often defined as "antiques." In their place, however, are mid- and late-20th-century furniture, equipment, and accessories, much of which has been mass produced, but which often has great charm and fine production values. Architectural salvage, along with secondhand office, hotel, and commercial fixtures, fittings, and equipment, can also be found more easily now, and these pages show how stylish they can look in a domestic setting.

The interiors displayed in this book are all real family homes, and their owners have often mixed flea-market finds with purchases from affordable chain stores, so they are genuinely houses that have been furnished on a budget. They've shared their secrets with us here, and have some great tips on making both contemporary and traditional interiors look good.

Above all, flea-market finds put the fun back into shopping, and you won't have to worry about getting a huge credit-card bill at the end. If you are furnishing a home, and you don't have much money, this book could save you a fortune—and you'll end up with an imaginative, individual, and stylish look.

Good luck!

Chapter 1

flea market
details

Shopping at flea markets can save you a lot of money. If you are furnishing your home on a budget you will get better quality and more individuality if you buy secondhand. Even if you have to restore something, you'll still be paying about half to two-thirds of what you would have paid for the same item new.

Be methodical. That is the key to finding a bargain. Always start at one end of a market or secondhand sale and work your way down each row, looking at every stall in turn from one end to the other. Don't dart about. The other top tip is to focus on just a few types of objects or have a mental list of what you're looking for. These pages will give you some good ideas about how to start.

Collections

Collecting is one of the best ways to improve your success rate when you start flea-market shopping. When you're faced with a pile of miscellaneous stuff of variable quality, it's easiest to look out for familiar shapes, colors, or designs. And as you learn more about a particular theme, you will be able to spot things that other people can't. Collections can be decorative or useful, or both.

Above: Take a simple pleasure in the design of everyday objects—here a grouping of old gauges, all picked up at markets and fairs, have an elegant retro feel. You could do the same with car badges, old maps, vintage sporting equipment, or old-fashioned tobacco or food cans and tins.

Left: A collection of necklaces and hats looks just as good when hung up as when worn. Costume jewelry is a good secondhand buy, but check that any clasps and clips work, as it would probably cost more than the piece is worth to repair.

Far left: A collection of bracelets in a large bowl. Jewelry doesn't have to be kept in boxes—rings, earrings, and bracelets are much easier to find in a shallow bowl, where they become part of the décor.

Left: Everyone hates throwing away their children's outgrown shoes—so line them up on a shelf or mantelpiece to create a charming exhibition of memorabilia.

Far left: Wooden toy ships found at fairs, markets, and sales. Old toys are nostalgic and decorative.

Left: Blue-and-white china is the perfect "starter" collection, because it's easy to spot, and varying patterns still look good together. The maker's marks on the bottom will tell you about china. You can also specialize in china by color, brand, or designer names (such as Wedgwood, Denby, or Susie Cooper) or type (stoneware, Staffordshire, chintz).

Storage and display

Boxes, tins, chests, jars, and baskets are all good flea-market finds, and when space is short it makes sense for storage to be decorative, too. There's also a trend toward not hiding everything away: Hats, jewelry, bags and purses, clothes, and kitchenalia can look great if displayed when not being used. Pick a theme, if you like, such as wicker, natural materials, or a color.

Above: A row of pretty frocks belonging to a little girl are hung on hangers hooked to the foot of her bed, adding a cheery floral touch to her bedroom.

Left: The increasing use of fitted cupboards in homes means that free-standing wardrobes and closets—especially big ones—can be picked up in secondhand stores and auctions quite cheaply. Stripping or painting an old wardrobe is a good way to update it—very often the heavy-looking, dark wooden ones can look completely different if either stripped back to the natural wood or painted a soft, light color, such as white or cream.

Far left: Many keen cooks collect wooden spoons, as it's useful to have a variety of sizes and shapes. Old wooden spoons have a wonderful patina, and they're no trouble to carry—you can always slip another one in, no matter how laden you are. Stacked together in jars, they look attractive and are easy to get hold of when you need one.

Left: Pretty wrapping paper has been used to line the shelves of a cupboard where a mix of flea-market china is displayed.

Far left: Old fruit boxes often come up for sale and they make great places to keep bottles as they can be tucked away.

Left: Wicker picnic baskets—and all other basketry—are well worth looking out for. Check the wear, as it may be difficult to repair broken clasps and frayed handles. Blankets, too, are always a brilliant find, especially if they are made of pure wool. If they look stained, the marks will often come out with dry cleaning.

Frames and mirrors

There is lots you can do with frames and mirrors, making them ideal flea-market buys. Look for poor-quality pictures with nice frames, because you can replace the image with mirror glass. Frames can be painted quickly and easily. You don't need any special paint or expertise—just use masking tape along the glass. Gilding, however, is a specialist craft—it's better to paint than to try to gild or re-gild.

Far left: This collection of mirrors shows how you can pull together different sizes and styles by painting the frames the same color. Hang a series of mirrors on the wall, like pictures, to add light to a hallway.

Left: Look out for similar shades of wooden or gilt mirrors when flea-market shopping so that they can be hung together. If you buy an old mirror with foxed or silvered mirror glass, never replace it with modern glass. This is the "character" of the mirror, and genuinely old mirrors are becoming increasingly sought after.

Far left: You can put mirror glass behind all sorts of things. Here Alex Legendre of i gigi, a lifestyle and fashion store based on England's south coast, has bought old clock cases, bleached the wood, and put mirror glass in place of the clock face.

Left: Buy old picture frames and put your own family photographs in them. Here a wide range of shapes and sizes looks good together because all the frames are white or black with black-and-white photos inside. You can have color photos converted into black and white quite easily.

Vases

You can find all sorts of lovely receptacles for flowers in flea markets, fairs, and thrift and charity stores. Pretty single glasses, pitchers, bowls, old bottles, medical glassware, jars—anything that holds water and has a secure base is a candidate. Our flea-market experts advise picking two or three quite specific themes to collect—for example, white pitchers, colored glass, or a particular make, such as Staffordshire china.

Right: A set of melamine egg cups can make a series of small table vases. Try just one bloom in each and cut stems very short.

Far right: A grouping of vases of different shapes and sizes works well, and you don't have to have flowers in all of them. Another trick would be to group several vases together and just put one or two blooms in each vase.

Right: Flea-market shopping means you can collect a large number of pitchers and vases in order to have the right receptacle for any bunch of flowers. Here the elaborate shape of a Victorian pitcher is best shown off with simple pink roses.

Far right: A classic everyday pitcher, used for milk or water, looks best with a mix of common garden flowers rather than a smart florist's bouquet.

Fabrics

Finding genuine vintage fabrics from the days before modern dyes is getting harder, but many companies manufacturing today reproduce old patterns, and these are now available secondhand, too. If you find a pattern you like, buy it, because you will always find a use for it. Cut partly damaged fabrics down to make pillows and cushions, bags, lampshades, and trims.

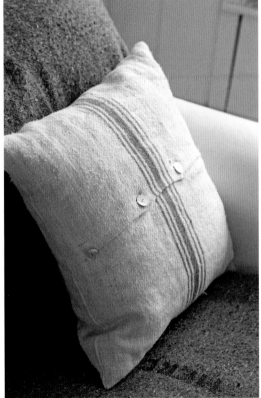

Above: This cushion is made from Hungarian sacking (probably a former mattress cover) bought from an antiques' market. Look for old mattress covers and sacks, and turn them into soft furnishings: They are hardwearing and charmingly rustic. As sacking is essentially cotton or linen, such materials are usually washable—try washing a small piece first to test it out.

Left: A delightful vintage fabric from a flea market makes a simple, lightweight window covering in a bedroom.

Far left: Interior designer Henny Tate used a small piece of antique French fabric to make a lampshade. Frames for homemade lampshades are sold on the internet—ideal if you have only a small scrap of usable fabric.

Left: Textile designer Helena Gavshon buys many of her vintage fabrics on her travels— the throw pillow cover is French. Fabrics are easy to pack so they're an ideal vacation buy.

Far left: If drapes, rugs, or bedspreads have become too torn or damaged, cut them down to make throw pillows and cushions. These ones came from Sanderson curtains that had been hanging for fifty years.

Left: Reuse fabrics in inventive ways: these are antique French linen sheets clipped to a curtain rail. Cotton Indian bedspreads would work, too. Sheets can also be turned into duvet covers or bedspreads, with a minimum of sewing.

Bathrooms and washrooms

Quirky flea-market finds make bathrooms and washrooms come alive. Be careful when buying salvaged bathtubs and basins. Iron bathtubs can be re-enamelled by specialists, but often chips and cracks cannot be repaired, and spare parts for older plumbing are hard to source. However, you can adapt furniture to make washstands, buy secondhand cabinets, and use walls as a place to display collections.

Above: Illustrator Mark Hearld chose a modern fitted basin to make the most of a small space, then used every inch of wall space to display tiles, plates, and a 1940s pull-along toy goose. The tiles and plates were made by potter Terry Shone and decorated by Mark, who also designed the asymmetrical wall cabinet. One side displays Staffordshire and 1950s slipware china, and the other provides practical bathroom storage.

Left: The basin and splashback are new sandstone, but the bowl sits on a chunk of reclaimed oak floorboard, suspended by invisible steel brackets. The distressed mirror above the handbasin was bought in a secondhand store in Denmark.

Far left: A built-in cistern gives you the option for an attractive display shelf above, and will also improve the proportions of a long, thin room.

Left: The little wall cupboard came from a chain store and a square of luxurious Cole and Son wallpaper is inset on the door, while on top are a Spanish medicine bottle from a market and a bowl bought through an online auction.

Far left: Tongue and groove paneling covers up pipework and makes a charming display shelf. The mirrored cabinet was found at a market.

Left: This traditional washstand would originally have held a bowl and pitcher, but it also lends itself to permanent plumbing. Check the height first: An inset bowl is lower than a bowl on top, which may not be comfortable for taller people, and you may have to lengthen the washstand legs.

Chapter 2
flea market
town

The greatest flea markets can be found in the world's major cities: Paris's
Marché aux Puces at Porte de Clignancourt, New York's Hell's Kitchen
on West 39th Street, London's New Caledonian Market in Bermondsey,
the Daytona Flea Market in Florida, the Rose Bowl Flea Market in the
UCLA Bruins football stadium in Pasadena, California, and Paddy's Flea
Market in Sydney's Chinatown, are just a few of them.

Cities are often a hodgepodge of cultures and races, as well as a hub of
artistic experimentation, so exotic or unusual markets can be found by
consulting local tourist information centers. If you live in a town or city
in a row of similar houses or a block of identical apartments, flea-market
finds help establish your own individual look, especially as city space is
often expensive, so your budget may be tight.

modern *eclectic*

This small city apartment belongs to hairdresser Kim Ward, and it has been decorated almost entirely with flea-market finds and internet auction bargains. Originally from New Zealand, she lives and works near London's Portobello and Golborne Road markets, so she looks round her favorite stalls and stores on her way to and from work. She also makes regular trips to the local markets and fairs, such as the big secondhand fair in Chiswick, west London. This kind of persistence always pays off. Anyone who despairs of finding bargains should locate a thrift or charity store that's on their regular route and make a point of going in whenever they have time to spare.

One complete wall in the living room is covered in a giant photo wall of a waterfall and trees. It was bought after a trawl online, as a single dramatic statement providing a wow factor for what is actually quite a small room. Kim had seen a few people use beach scenes, but decided that greenery would be both more dramatic and natural. It arrived in eight delicate pieces and needed carefully wallpapering up.

A huge L-shaped sofa, bought secondhand from a store on Portobello Road (before the latest fire retardancy regulations tightened up the resale of upholstered furniture), is the main piece of furniture in the room. It seats several people and opens up into a giant bed. It is covered with cushions that Kim has picked up from fairs, or that she has made from scraps of velvet or silk. She advises dry cleaning or taking precautions against moths when you buy secondhand fabrics to avoid potentially ruining all your own clothes and furniture.

Above left: Kim always keeps an eye out for a good mirror when she's shopping for bargains. This one reflects the woodland waterfall photo wall opposite.
Left: A wooden vessel from the Chiswick Car Boot Sale.
Right: Grand gestures make rooms memorable: The giant photo wall and huge L-shaped sofa both make a dramatic statement. The "coffee table" is a Chinese lacquer chest, which doubles as storage for DVDs. Chinoiserie, or Chinese-influenced furniture, has gone in and out of fashion since the 17th century, so there are often affordable examples to be found in auction houses. And since the 1990s genuine Chinese antiques have been imported into the US, Europe, and Australia in large quantities and at reasonable prices.

classic *contemporary*

Above left: Kim spent a long time looking for exactly the right cabinet to display her shoes in, and she found the painting above the cabinet at a fair.

Above center: If it's pretty, show it off. Even secondhand shoes can become ornaments.

Above right: This collection of glass vases was bought from a retro shop in Notting Hill in London.

Right: The glass easel table, given to Kim as a present, is at the opposite end of the living room. The chairs are chain-store versions of the famous Eero Saarinen dining chairs, and were found at a fair. The gilt mirror came from London's Portobello Road market.

Kim's dining area shows how well modern furniture goes with traditional dark woods and gilt. In a combined living room-dining room, too much dark wood might be oppressive, so the clean lines of the modern chairs and table create space and light. She buys instinctively, recognizing the shapes and colors she likes, but there are names you can look for in terms of modern designer furniture: Charles and Ray Eames, Eero Saarinen, Arne Jacobsen, Harry Bertoia, Ercol, G-Plan, and Ron Arad, as well as almost anything Scandinavian. Look for vintage or furniture shops that in your area that specialize in "mid-20th-century modern" to get to know styles and prices. Some designs are still in production, and mid-century modern furniture can often be found at auctions and garage or car boot sales.

Kim knew she wanted to have her shoes on show, so she waited for years to find the perfect cabinet for them, and eventually walked past this one at London's Golborne Road street market. Always think about how you could combine storage and display in a small space—if you have a lovely collection of shoes or jewelry, using it as a feature instead of hiding it in cupboards means you can enjoy it every day.

small space *tricks*

In a small kitchen, fitted units make the most of every inch. Kim has been enterprising about this, too—she contacted the Formica company directly to order the bench seating and kitchen work surface directly from them to her own design. The banquettes have storage beneath, and the countertop looks smart because it is a little deeper than average. The stepped cupboards on the wall are another clever touch—you don't need all your cupboards to be deep, and the row of smaller cupboards beneath the larger ones makes the work surface seem more spacious. The choice of the dark wood-look Formica picks up on both the modern theme and her dark wood furniture.

Kim's philosophy is to keep backgrounds and large items neutral—here, the use of lots of white creates a feeling of light and space. She then uses accent colors as highlights, as shown here by the green lamps, which came from IKEA. The bench seating, like the L-shaped sofa, can accommodate a surprising number of people, and the table has a useful flap for when she has extra guests.

Left: Kim and her daughter visit India every year, and the elephant and the figure of Ganesha—the Hindu household God, who helps smooth your way in life—come from Indian markets. More character comes from the vintage elements: the clock, which is from a secondhand fair, and the plaster of Paris mirror from Portobello Road market.

Above left: Kim's household scales are one of the few items in her home that she bought new from a department store. Note the way the stepped cupboards create a sense of space on the work surface.

Above right: Her collection of charming storage jars was from the Chiswick Car Boot Sale.

Kim could be described as the "car boot queen," but she doesn't necessarily strike a hard bargain. If a garage sale or car boot fair is a regular event in your neighborhood and you go to it often, the chances are that you will get to know people. She feels that this makes for a relatively honest trading environment. Most people will mention if something is damaged in any way—although do ask them—and her philosophy is, "if I think the price is right, I don't bargain."

The photographs above show the range of her collecting interests. She has been collecting Royalty-inspired mugs for a long time, "well before the Will and Kate marriage," and finds these fairly easy to find. "Most of mine come from the Golborne Road market."

The vase on the windowsill on page 26 is typical of a garage sale find: Every sale can be guaranteed to yield at least one good vase. In order to make sense of the clutter and to end up with a collection that feels cohesive, some people concentrate on a particular design style—

such as Scandinavian modern, country, or traditional floral—or a particular medium—glass, pottery, earthenware, or bone china. You could also choose to concentrate on a certain color or good shapes and sizes for flower arranging. Others use more random criteria, such as only buying items priced at less than $20 (£10).

You don't always have to buy secondhand to get a vintage feel. Many chain stores include classic and traditional designs among their lines—good design doesn't date—so anyone on a budget will be able to find something that suits at a price they can afford, such as this classic light from IKEA. Lighting is one area where it is more sensible to buy new, because electrical standards are constantly being upgraded, and you can't guarantee that a piece of electrical equipment is safe or will work, unless you buy it from a shop.

Once you've decided on your own theme, tell everyone about it. You'll find other people spot "your" china, and give you more as presents.

Opposite page left: Mugs from Kim's collection of Royal memorabilia. It's fun to collect everyday items like these, because they are so evocative of a particular time and place. The owner of the antiques shop where Kim buys them knows that she loves them so keeps them aside for her when they come in—another reason why it's worth calling into such stores often, and building up a relationship with the staff.

Opposite page right: A vintage-style china cake stand adds atmosphere to a party. Home baking has had a resurgence in popularity, and it's even better with traditional china to match. There's also a growing fashion for vintage-themed events, such as weddings or birthday parties, so it's fun to collect dishes and plates that you can bring out on special occasions.

Above left: Both the plaster of Paris mirror, which is a reproduction of an antique version, and the green lamp were bought new. Kim likes to hang her mirrors high to add light to the room, rather than to see her own reflection.

Above right: The elephants are mementoes of Kim's vacations in India with her daughter. Although Kim admits that she sometimes gets "caught up in the moment" and buys a trinket she regrets, she thinks that buying abroad is extra-special because whatever you buy will remind you of your travels.

flea market *glamour*

This gorgeous bedroom is unashamedly feminine, with its gold and gilt boudoir atmosphere. Kim lived in Australia for ten years, where she fell in love with the designs of Florence Broadhurst, a well-known designer from the 1920s. The rights to her designs have now been bought by Australian company, Signature Prints, who ship all over the world, but they are not cheap. So Kim hunted long and hard to find something equivalent more in line with her budget, and, perhaps for the first time in her life, had to admit defeat.

However, one advantage of doing most of your shopping in flea markets is that you can save enough to make a few stunning investments. An expensive wallpaper, for example, creates the atmosphere of a room, setting the scene for the bargains.

Above left: Kim had the fitted wardrobe made, then added the moldings herself and aged them with boot polish.
Above right: The antique bedside chest perfectly echoes the gold wallpaper.
Right: Kim's bedroom is a cunning mix of vintage and chain-store buys, achieving an opulent and romantic effect on a budget. The bed is a reproduction French-style bed from The French Bed Company and the bed linen is a mix of chain-store sheets with 1920s and 1940s eiderdowns bought at fairs. The chandelier lampshade, drapes, and rug were all bought from chain stores.

Having saved money elsewhere, Kim ordered her dream Florence Broadhurst wallpaper. However, she had more flea-market success with the gilt bedside table. She had spotted a similar one in an expensive antique shop, but kept looking, hoping to find a cheaper equivalent. Eventually she found this one and paid about a quarter of the price of the one she'd originally seen. This is why it is so important to learn about what you're looking for. Browsing through upmarket antique shops is not a waste of time, because you'll soon be able to recognize something good when you see it buried in a pile of junk.

Modern built-in wardrobes and closets might seem out of place in this room, but they are great space-savers and provide maximum storage. Kim had the cupboards built, then gave them an antique look by buying the moldings and trim from a builders' merchants, gluing them on herself, and then buffing them up with boot polish to age it.

Flea-market shopping doesn't stop at china, glass, and vases. Kim finds that markets and fairs are excellent sources of secondhand handbags, shoes, scarves, and jewelry, and she likes to display her most beautiful specimens. Novelty handbags from the 1950s —particularly those from the US—are becoming increasingly collectable, but you can still find bargains if you look for them.

In the 1950s the idea of having a different bag or purse for each outfit heralded the new consumerism. Mass-market manufacturing techniques brought ultra-elegant coordinated fashion, and the bags of that time are now very collectable. Companies took advantage of new materials, such as acrylic glass, as well as more traditional ones, such as wicker, fabric, or wood, to make bags and purses fun. The US manufactured most of the best designs of the time, although there are also European equivalents. Look out for those with themes, such as strawberries, poodles or other animals, flowers, birds, or seaside motifs. Names to collect include Midas of Miami, the New York firm Llewellyn, Wilardy, Charles S. Kahn, Rialto, and the Nantucket Lightship Company. Any quirky purse with "Florida" or "Miami" on its label may well be a 1950s original.

Left: Jewelry, shoes, and bags were all bought at markets, but the acrylic glass chair came from a sale at The Conran Shop.
Above right: One of Kim's collection of vintage handbags, which she likes to display rather than hide away.
Below right: Single wine glasses cost next to nothing secondhand, and can be used as little vases.

smart *townhouse*

City fabrics are luxurious—velvets, silks, and cashmere—and city patterns are stylized. This is not a large room but it shows how powerful the use of color can be in creating a sophisticated effect. Some people might have been tempted to paint it white to increase the sense of space and light, but many designers believe that it's better to do the opposite, especially if you mainly use a room in the evenings. This is the case here, as the owners work long hours and are rarely home during the day. Instead of trying to make it lighter and brighter, textile designer Helena Gavshon decided to embrace the room's potential for strong, rich colors to create a stylish and smart—yet still cozy—environment.

The starting point is the rich purple wallpaper from Neisha Crosland, which is echoed in the purple velvet sofa. In a small room, too much contrast would look busy and make the room look smaller. She bought the sofa privately from a friend—although fire retardancy regulations have made secondhand sales difficult in some countries, this is still allowed—and re-covered it with fabric from Linwood. The throw pillows are all auction or eBay finds, with the fabric for the velvet pillows coming from Paris.

Above left: The pillows were made from fabrics from markets and secondhand stores.
Above right: The colorful little box was a present and came from a Russian market.
Right: The pine chest of drawers came from a secondhand furniture shop, and the painting above, by Mary Fedden, was bought at auction.
Overleaf left: The mantelpiece is adorned with a toy car, which came from a London market, candlesticks, which were a gift, and a vintage black-and-white family photo.
Overleaf right: The chair was re-covered with fabric from Warris Vianni, as was the footstool, which came from the Portobello Road market. The pine corner cupboard was an auction buy, and the paintings were bought through John Bennett Fine Paintings.

paint *plus*

White-painted walls are perennially fresh and fashionable, but by painting the floor white, too, the maximum amount of light is reflected and the room looks bigger and brighter. In towns, where houses tend to be smaller and narrower, painted floors work well. The all-white paint treatment, as seen here, blurs the definition between wall and floor, which is why rooms can look wider than they are.

But paint isn't just for walls and floors. This sofa was found in a "bargain basement." Most stores have a small section where soiled or slightly damaged goods are sold off at hugely discounted prices, and this was a white leather sofa that had become very marked in store. Few people would think of painting soft furniture, but this dramatic red is not the result of reupholstery or buying slipcovers. The owner transformed it by painting it, seat cushions and all, with a bright red acrylic paint, mixing the paint with a polymer to make it more flexible. It has survived several years, although occasionally flecks of paint wear off. She just gets out her paintbrush and touches it up.

It takes a certain amount of courage to paint unusual items, but if you haven't paid much for them in the first place, then you have much less to lose. Here, you could have experimented on the underside of the seat cushions to see if you'd got the consistency right for giving it a certain amount of wear, before going ahead to paint the whole sofa.

Left: The red-painted sofa sits beneath unusual shelving. This is, in fact, the top half of a dresser, which has been detached and hung on the wall with a charming collection of little sculptures.
Above far left: This guitar is not only for decoration— it is also played.
Above left: One of a collection of "fencing" sculptures.
Above: The black chair was also bought very cheaply because one leg was wobbly, but it hasn't been a problem to fix it. If you're prepared to do minor repairs on furniture, you can often find a good bargain. The cabinet in the right-hand corner is an old office filing cabinet, which was being thrown out.

painting *floors*

This is the hallway of the house featured on the previous two pages, and its owner's clever ways with paint continue across the floorboards. At first glance, the green, yellow, and terracotta design on the floor appears to be tiled, but in fact she photographed the distinctive Moorish tiling when she visited Alhambra in Spain, and copied the design onto her own floorboards, hand-painting it herself. You may need something of an artist's eye and a steady hand to paint your floor freehand, but a charming repeat pattern like this would also lend itself to stenciling. As you can see, heavy areas of wear on painted floors do fade, but it is not difficult to patch up from time to time.

The stairs are also painted. The owner first painted them white, but decided she didn't really like it, so she repainted them powder blue. Eventually, she decided she preferred this soft duck-egg blue instead, so this is their third coat. However, as the top layer of paint wears, glimpses of the powder blue and white are revealed, creating an attractive layered effect.

Above left and above: The pattern on the floor was hand painted, copying tiling seen in the Alhambra, the 14th-century palace and fortress in Granada, Spain. Moorish tile design, which evolved over the centuries from the interweaving of Islamic and Christian cultures, is renowned for its abstract patterns and strong colors. The patterns lend themselves well to stenciling.

Right: The standing sculpture is by Sophie Dickens. Family photographs are "crowded up" on the wall: "Crowding up" is an old trick of antique addicts, because a grouping of things is often much more effective than just one or two items hung or displayed on their own (see also page 131).

Chapter 3
flea market
country

The essence of country style is encapsulated in flowers and floral patterns, mismatched furniture, open fires, and range cookers. Colors reflect the earth, meadows, or sky. The flea market is the perfect hunting ground for this look, because distressed wooden furniture, classic china, and faded fabrics all make homes look as if they have been lived in and loved for generations by the same family.

The country look is for humble materials without designer names: seek out enamelware and tin, copper pans, fabrics that can be cut down and reused—such as mattress ticking or good-quality secondhand curtains and drapes—basketware, traditional china and glass, pictures with animals or flowers, and vintage kitchenalia.

kitchen *reclamation*

This delightful kitchen (along with the rooms featured up to page 55) belongs to Henny Tate, an interior designer who specializes in creating relaxing, stylish, family-friendly interiors. She places a special emphasis on reusing and reclaiming wherever she can, mixing flea-market and chain-store finds with classic and contemporary design.

There are lots of ways to acquire kitchen units, as people often tend to take out even good-quality kitchens because they don't like the style. Here the drawers came via the internet, the countertop was the top of a pool table, the doors came from a chain store, and the table was specially made from cedar that had been recycled from the sea defences in the English seaside town of Hastings.

It's not too difficult to pull such different elements together. If you've got, for example, a chest of drawers and a cupboard, both different heights, you may be able to cut down the legs of one or add a little height to the other using small blocks of wood. Then you could paint it all the same color and run a countertop across the top to unify the look. You can mix purpose-built kitchen units with pieces of furniture, and old with new, but make sure that everything is sturdy, with drawers and doors opening easily. Kitchen cupboards and units from the 1950s and 1960s—and later—can be found relatively cheaply in secondhand stores, at house

Above left: This country kitchen makes the most of wood, with two rustic floor-to-ceiling cupboards with shelving in between. The table is made of recycled cedar, by Carbon, a company specializing in reclaimed wood, and the mismatched chairs came from antique and secondhand stores. The pendant light is French.
Above center: The walls are not tongue-and-groove, but planking, made to order by a joiner. Below the clock—which was a wedding present—there is a pull-down cupboard concealing the microwave. The slate countertop came from an old pool table.
Above right: The cow painting is by artist Celia Lewis and the wall light is from vintage-inspired lighting company Original BTC.

clearances, or on eBay. Mending furniture and putting it together is well within the capabilities of a good amateur handyman, but an expert is needed for both the plumbing and the electrics.

Look out for pieces that can be broken up and remade. These can include large, heavy pieces of furniture, such as this pool-table top (used as a work surface), church pews, which can be re-cut into tables, or wooden beams. It is not cheap to get furniture made to order, even if you use reclaimed materials, but it can be worthwhile, and the cost is often no higher than buying good-quality furniture from a store.

Find joiners, furniture designers, and craftsmen by asking around. Start by checking the internet or your local telephone directory, or asking at craft stores and galleries where furniture is sold. Try to find more than one, so you can compare their prices and approach. Ask to see examples (or photographs) of their work and for a rough estimate of costs. Before going ahead, get an exact written quotation, and be clear about what you need the furniture for and how hardwearing it needs to be.

Above left: The window shade is cut down from a larger piece of old fabric, and the glass vases, pitcher, and decanters are from a variety of sources: gifts, secondhand stores, and auctions.
Above right: The three mismatched chairs came from a secondhand store. The fabric frieze is an Indian bed hanging.
Overleaf left: The hen throw pillow was printed from a painting by Celia Lewis and the bench cushion was made from Hungarian sacking—which is hardwearing and washable—bought at an antique market.
Overleaf right: Behind the reclaimed cedar kitchen table, you can see the kitchen units, which were put together from a mix of sources. The Aga oven was bought secondhand.

rustic *and simple*

Henny Tate's charming room shows how the country look relies on simplicity and texture, with soft paint colors—bright modern whites are avoided. The uneven beam, walls, and ceiling show that this is an old country cottage, but even if you live in a modern house, you can evoke similar country cottage style by keeping an eye out for architectural finds—such as cottage-style doors or paneling—in markets, salvage yards, secondhand stores, or on eBay. And if you are renovating any part of your own house, keep or reuse anything you can.

Traditionally, houses were built reusing as much material as possible. Before chain stores mass-produced doors, windows, and other fittings, they were routinely reused from other properties. Any building that was demolished was stripped of anything useful first. Even windows can be refitted, and it is also possible to buy paneling, and have it recut to fit your room. Just one caveat—if you are covering walls with paneling, be careful that you are not covering up any damp problems, because they will only get worse.

Left: The row of colorful baskets along the windowsill came from a chain store and the low child's desk was a present from a neighbor. The small children's chairs are a mix of old and new: one from IKEA and the other a family heirloom.
Right: The sofa is a classic style, and can be found either new or secondhand, and at every price point. The navy throw came from a French interiors store called Merci, and the throw pillows were made from recycled Hungarian sacking.

transformation *tips*

Almost everything in this cottage bedroom has been transformed by the use of paint or antique fabric. Think carefully before you paint an old piece of furniture—sometimes you may be destroying its charm. However, when appropriate, paint is one of the most effective ways to turn a flea-market find into exactly the piece you've been looking for. The chest of drawers and the bedside table have both been painted to harmonize with the room. Prepare surfaces carefully, scrubbing, then sanding, and use good-quality paintbrushes. Adding new handles can also revive a chest of drawers.

The bed has been reupholstered with vintage fabric and the corona above it is little more than a shelf with antique linen sheets attached to it. Drapes and curtains, sheets, and bedspreads can be found in flea markets, but are often worn or marked. Cut them down to use over smaller areas: upholster bedheads or make pillows and cushions, window shades, or ornamental drapes.

Left: Flowers from the garden, displayed in an old jam jar, add a pretty touch.

Above left: The old chest of drawers was inherited, then repainted in Farrow & Ball's Pavilion Gray and given new handles. The blue rug was a wedding present.

Above right: The blue bedside table was originally in an ugly, modern, "orange" pine. Painting it a soft color gave it an antique country look. The throw pillow is made from a scrap of antique fabric from textile dealer Elizabeth Baer.

Right: The bed was bought via the internet, and then reupholstered. The corona above was made of antique French linen sheets, gathered to make drapes, with an ornamental trim added. The rug was bought at auction.

buying *tricks*

The view through these two doors shows how just one or two splashes of color from fabric or rugs can brighten a room. On the left Henny Tate uses her daughter's dresses as decoration—hanging them off the end of the bed with pretty hangers—and on the right a brilliantly colored rug, bought from eBay, transforms the bathroom.

Buying rugs and textiles on the internet and through online auctions isn't always easy, because you can't see the product's true colors on your computer screen. Sometimes, if a fabric is branded, and you know the brand, you can make a guess—or, if it's a very good price, it may be worth taking a risk, and trying to resell it again if it turns out to be not what you hoped it was. If you're buying a rug, Henny Tate cautions you to check as to how much black you can see in the design: If you want a clear or bright effect, the less black the better. She also believes that now is a good time to buy rugs at auction, where you can see the colors properly. Persian rugs are relatively unfashionable at the moment so they are being sold at good prices.

While stores often let you exchange a rug if it turns out to be wrong for your room, you can't do this when you're buying online or at an auction, so be careful about measurements. Mark out where you want the rug to go and measure it carefully, working out how much bigger or smaller you'd be happy for it to be. Otherwise, you can find that when you get your rug home, it is dramatically wrong for the space! Areas of wear and tear can be repaired, but it's a professional job, and will be expensive. You may be able to conceal the worn part under furniture, but be aware that if bare threads are exposed, then they are a trip hazard. A very worn rug, if beautiful, is often worth buying and cutting down to make a large cushion or ottoman.

Left: A view through two doors to a child's bedroom and the bathroom. The French bed came from an antique shop and is decorated with the child's pretty dresses. The blue stool came from an antiques' arcade, the little chair was a present from Henny's sister, and the rug was bought from eBay. Henny buys old picture frames and uses them for family photographs, seen here hung between the two doors.

flea market *bathroom*

The truth is that major items in a bathroom, such as the basin, bath, and shower, are often better if they're bought new. But there are exceptions, so it's worth looking at vintage basins. If they're in good condition, they can be plumbed in with new faucets or taps. If the porcelain is cracked or very stained, there's often little that can be done to renovate them. Henny Tate also warns against buying old basins when plumbing has been welded in, because getting them out damages the basin and it may be impossible to buy washers for them.

Henny bought the clawfoot bathtub as a modern reproduction, but secondhand cast-iron enamel bathtubs can be effectively resurfaced for about 40 percent of the cost of buying new. Specialist bathtub restoration companies use sprays to recoat the bathtub to bring up its shine, or to patch up worn holes in the enamel. A bathtub needs recoating if you can feel or see pitted areas, where the enamel surface has worn away to reveal the iron underneath. Give the bathtub a good clean first, so that you can see which marks are caused by permanent staining or wear and whether you can eliminate them with cleaning. However, check that the cleaning agent you use is suitable for use on enamel—the wrong cleaner can cause permanent damage.

Left: The flea-market look is achieved with a set of botanical Victorian prints that were bought at auction, a pretty, old mug, and vintage shelf-brackets. It's difficult to find good working basins secondhand, but many mid-range bathroom companies do excellent historic designs, so you should be able to find a new basin and plumbing—such as the ones on the left—to give you the effect you want at a reasonable price.

Above left: Before buying an iron bathtub, check that your floor can take the weight. Henny Tate chose a modern reproduction because hers couldn't.

Above right: Old French glass storage jars are filled with shells, and the window shade is made with an inexpensive offcut of material by top fabric company Vanderhurd.

vintage *colors*

Above: Helena collects two kinds of pans: cream Le Creuset pans on the lower shelf and Le Pentole on the top shelf. Both are high-quality cookware, and still in production, but they are good secondhand names to look for as they are exceptionally hardwearing and long lasting.

Above center: The knitted tea cozy dates from the 1950s and was bought in London's famous Portobello Road market, and the teacups were a present from a friend.

Above right: Old 1920s pitchers from Portobello Road make great holders for kitchen utensils.

The house on the next twelve pages belongs to textile designer Helena Gavshon, who specializes in sourcing antique fabrics from 1850 to 1950, then adapting the designs for fashion and homeware companies. Her clients range from top couture names to chain stores. She travels constantly, seeking out flea markets and antique stores around the world, from the US to France, Britain, and Japan. She never passes a thrift or charity store without going in for a quick look to see what they may have available.

Helena says that it's generally becoming harder to find old textiles, and that prices continue to rise, but that old patterns are being reused. You may find copies of vintage fabrics at reasonable prices in chain stores, flea markets, and sales. An antique fabric design she picks out in Japan or France may end up on designer curtains in a wealthy home in London, then, when the owner of the house redecorates again, the curtains are sold secondhand through an auction room, online, or in a secondhand store. The cycle is continuous, and there are opportunities for everyone.

Helena's technique for finding something wonderful among a pile of ordinary fabrics is to focus on the colors, and how they harmonize. The same goes for china, and even art. That's why she's chosen a soft, light-reflecting pink for the walls of

her own kitchen-dining room, as it is a shade that both absorbs and reflects light, and it works well with most other colors. It's warmer than white, and just as flexible. By taking a similar tone of color over the kitchen units and shelves as well as the walls, she has created a calm, welcoming, and pretty feel, and one that is simple enough to sustain an ever-changing collection of differently patterned and colored fabric, china, and glass. In a dining room or kitchen, she suggests, the table is a major presence, so by changing the tablecloth you can really change the feel of the room.

Helena's top advice for shopping in flea markets is to "buy what you like, and even if you don't have room for it, it'll find a place. But always be prepared to wade through a lot of junk." Almost everything in her house comes from a flea market, a thrift or charity shop, an auction, or a sale. It's difficult to find complete sets of things—such as chairs, dinner plates, or glasses—in good condition, but you may be able to repair the damaged items or collect sets piecemeal.

Above left: The pottery mugs are over a hundred years old and very pretty, but too fragile to use. If you do use old pottery, wash by hand as dishwasher detergents will make the colors fade.

Above: Vintage colanders are popular, and occasionally seem wildly overpriced, but you can still find a bargain if you keep an eye open.

Overleaf left: The soft pink (Dulux Pink Nevada) of the walls is very close to the tone of the units, woodwork, and shelving, creating a very calm backdrop for vintage finds.

Overleaf right: The fitted kitchen is by Plain English, a company specializing in simple, pared-down design and authentic detail. The paint color is from Dulux's Khaki Mist range.

mix *not match*

Mixing, rather than matching, has long been fashionable, but it is most successful when there are a few almost invisible rules, as seen in the dining end of Helena Gavshon's kitchen-dining room. Here the set of dining chairs establishes an approximate chair-back height, which the two additional chairs on the side (pulled up when more than six are eating at the table) follow. The armchairs are not the same, but both have a laidback traditional "club" feel, and are upholstered harmoniously in soft, pretty blues. The pictures on the back wall range from nursery rhyme depictions to Paula Rego prints, but are all given a wide white border and a thin, contemporary black frame.

One of the armchairs was bought in a sale, and is by top British furniture maker George Smith, and the other was secondhand. In some countries there are now tight regulations about fire retardancy and secondhand furniture, so it can be difficult to buy in stores or at auction, but there are no restrictions on private sales. Big pieces of furniture, such as sofas and armchairs, are often passed down when people move house—quite rightly, few want to throw away such major items, but they can be difficult to sell. So keep an eye out for friends or relatives with unwanted furniture! Some countries also have free exchange schemes—The Freecycle Network began in Arizona, and has now spread worldwide to more than 85 countries, including Britain, Germany, and Australia.

Reupholstering a sofa or armchair is not cheap—aim to allow around 50 percent of what it would cost you to buy something similar brand new—so it is worth doing only when the furniture itself is well made and of good quality.

Left: The right-hand armchair is secondhand and has been reupholstered in Celia Birtwell fabric. The two chairs along the right-hand wall have both been painted—Helena's advice is to "live with a chair for a while before painting it. And use sample pots to try different colors— paint them directly on the chair itself." The wicker chair is painted in matt lilac paint, and the pink chair is an old school chair recoated in gloss paint.

China is the ultimate mix-not-match collectable. Gone are the days when young brides-to-be ordered complete dinner sets, to be brought out only for special occasions. Today's tables combine fine china and porcelain with colorful pottery, chain-store plates with vintage designs. True flea-market addicts will have piles of plates and pitchers on every surface. Just as gardeners sometimes appreciate it when a plant dies—so that they can discover a new one—china addicts don't mind if the odd plate gets broken because it's an excuse for another hunt around a fair or sale.

Helena Gavshon picks out just pieces that she likes, but others prefer to specialize in certain areas, and like to find out more about particular makes of china. Fine bone china and porcelain are the "smart" end, while everyday pottery is called earthenware or stoneware. Since the 18th century, most makers stamp their marks on the bottom. China marks can be researched on the internet to find out more about what you're buying. Fine china can be very expensive, but you can collect good specimens at very low prices from garage or car boot sales and thrift or charity shops.

Above left: Make the most of your china collection in a cupboard with glass doors—the ideal compromise between being able to see your plates and keeping them dust free.
Above right: With the growth in popularity of tea bags, vintage teapots are easy to find and usually very cheap at fairs and markets. And you can use them, too, even if you don't like making tea with loose tea—a couple of tea bags will often go further in a pot with more hot water added. This two-tone pottery style was popular in the first half of the 20th century, and the floral printed side plates date from the 1930s, too.

Once you start to recognize a particular name and its typical designs, you will spot it easily in a pile of junk, quickly notching up bargains. Most of the most famous brands can be found in markets all over the world, regardless of their country of origin.

Fine china brands include Lenox and Haviland from the US, and Wedgwood, Royal Doulton, Royal Worcester, Spode, and Burslem from the UK. Portmeirion and Denby are among the well known pottery names in the UK, along with Metlox, Blue Ridge, and Fiesta in the US. There are some wonderful European brands, too: look for Rosenthal from Germany, Limoges porcelain from France (Limoges is an area where a number of companies manufacture fine porcelain), along with the cheerful French peasant designs of Quimper and Gien. From the mid-20th century there was an explosion of interest in Scandinavian design, so you might want to specialize in china and pottery from Denmark or Sweden (try Royal Copenhagen or Bing & Grondahl). In Australia, some of the most famous names include Bendigo, J. Campbell Pty, Mashman Brothers, Bakewell, Melrose Australian Ware, and Diana Ware.

Above left: Helena uses vintage fabrics to make cushions for her dining chairs, but not every chair cushion is the same. The tablecloth also comes from her collection of vintage and secondhand fabrics.

Above center: Helena used gift wrapping paper from textile design brand Neisha Crosland to line the shelves of her china cabinet, and the delicate designs and colors provide an ideal foil for her collection of vintage plates. The white plates are Wedgwood, and the others are a mix of fine porcelain and pottery.

Above right: Trays are another good thing to be found in thrift or charity shops and secondhand markets. This is a little French tray, but you could collect trays in wood, tin, enamel, or wicker as well. Traditional cut-glass salt-and-pepper sets, often known as a cruet, are also collectables: First widely available from the 19th century onward, you can find salt-and-pepper dishes and shakers in pottery, china, silver, or glass, or even as novelty items, such as pairs of cats or cartoon characters.

vintage-style *wallpaper*

Helena Gavshon also sources vintage wallpapers on her travels, and has used them in several rooms in her house. These charming prints, with their stylized flowers and leaves, give her town house the air of a country cottage. She says that, although wallpapers from the 1960s, 1970s, and 1980s still hang well, it is usually difficult to use much older ones as they become brittle with age and can tear too easily.

You don't often see rolls of vintage wallpapers at markets, garage or car boot sales, or in thrift or charity shops, but the internet, particularly eBay, is a very good source of secondhand wallpapers. These may be leftovers from a job—in which case they'll be new patterns currently in manufacture—or they may be the result of someone clearing out the very back of an old warehouse or stockroom. You are unlikely to find more than half a dozen rolls of any particular pattern at any one time, though, so this is a decorating strategy for smaller rooms, or perhaps if you want to have just one wall wallpapered.

Above left: The wallpaper is a design from top British wallpaper company Osborne & Little, the desk is from a market in Suffolk, England, the chair is designed by Mark Meynard, and the picture was a present from Helena's mother.
Above right: Helena bought the mirror in London's Portobello Road market and painted it, while the table is a modern replica of an old-fashioned table.

As with fabrics, it is difficult to judge wallpaper colors accurately when you see only a small snapshot on screen, but Helena finds that descriptions from sellers are usually reliable. If you know a particular brand, you will have a clearer idea, but there's an element of pot luck, adding to the excitement of bargain shopping.

There is a slight difference between true vintage wallpapers, manufactured thirty or more years ago, and long-established patterns made by companies still in production, or historic styles that have been revived. Some companies, such as Hamilton Weston (seen here above right), specialize in reproducing historic wallpapers from scraps found in old houses or replicating old designs. These can be bought new or in sales, but if you admire a particular company's work, it is worth keeping an eye out for when odd rolls of their wallpapers come onto the internet at a good price. As with all flea-market bargains, persistence and luck are the most important factors in finding a good deal. Look for closing-down sales or particular brands, and one day you will spot a pattern that you really fall in love with.

Above left: Bright beads and bangles pick out the colors of the cushions on the bed.
Above right: The wallpaper is designed by Martha Armitage and is from Hamilton Weston, who specialize in reviving vintage designs.
Overleaf left: A delightful folkloric rocking chair bought in an antique shop. It is echoed with the pillow, which is also made out of fabric with a similarly folk-inspired pattern.
Overleaf right: Vintage quilts sourced on Helena Gavshon's travels cover the bed. Genuinely old quilts are becoming increasingly hard to find, but keep an eye out for secondhand modern reproductions. All-cotton bedcovers can be washed, but use low temperatures.

country *kitchen*

The country look is achieved here with a minimal run of fitted units, and the rest of the kitchen is furnished with free-standing pieces and open shelves. The units along the side wall, the wall-hung cupboard, and the shelves were all made by a local carpenter, and, provided you know what you want, this can be cheaper than buying a professionally fitted kitchen.

The kitchen table came from a local auction, and is typical of the kind of furniture that can be picked up quite cheaply if you're prepared to hunt around. The steel cabinet was a cunning buy—it's actually an old 1950s catering unit for keeping food hot. It shows how you should forget "labels" when you're bargain-hunting and focus on what things might look like in a different context. Stores, offices, and restaurants regularly throw furniture out, or send it to secondhand stores when they're refitting, and such pieces will look very different in a domestic environment.

Above left: The cabinet is a 1950s catering hot cupboard, but is now used to store dishes and plates.

Above right: The two watercolors are by artist Julia Dickens, and the orange colander came from Habitat in the 1960s—and is considered an "heirloom" by its owner! Some of the pans came from London's Brick Lane market.

Left: This holder for newly laid eggs was carved out of a solid piece of oak, which was then waxed.

Right: The open shelves were handbuilt and their different shelf heights maximize storage. The wall cupboard makes a good place for a useful work light, and a rail across the kitchen window is used for hanging kitchen utensils, acquired from many different sources. Look out for vintage kitchenalia—it is inexpensive, practical, and cleans up well.

The countertop was recycled from a school chemistry laboratory. Schools, too, are a source of recycled goodies for eagle-eyed flea-market hunter, since schools equipped in the mid-20th century often used solid, enduring materials. Ask if things are being thrown away. Look out for old parquet flooring, teak from the science laboratories, and old wooden desks. If you use teak for a kitchen work surface you will need a professional drill to create the necessary holes for plumbing and draining grooves, but if you don't have one, a local carpenter should be able to make them for you.

A big kitchen sink makes life easier for the cook—and also for the washer-up, as roasting pans and big dishes are much easier to wash up in a larger sink. But they are expensive and difficult to find when new. Recycling is an excellent route. Big kitchen sinks can still be found in reclamation centers, or discarded from schools, institutions, and hospitals when they're being refitted, but it's best to buy the faucets or taps new. Most mid-market ranges have classic styles that will look good with this type of sink.

Above: All the kitchen implements are secondhand. Kitchenalia can be picked up cheaply at almost any garage or car boot sale.

Above right: It can be difficult to find the right size message board for a kitchen—this one is a sheet of MDF, painted with blackboard paint.

Below right, left to right: The open shelves were made to order by a local carpenter, and show how decorative the packaging of even humble items can be; this is a new faucet in a classic style; a storage tin, picked up some years ago from a French market.

Chapter 4
flea market
modern

There's a misconception that if you decorate your home with vintage and flea-market furniture, you'll end up with a traditional or old-fashioned look. However, this is not necessarily the case—since the 1950s and 1960s, well-designed contemporary furniture has been mass produced and is today available secondhand at very affordable prices. When hunting through markets, auctions, and secondhand stores, look for anything Scandinavian, mass-market copies of 20th-century designers, office and store furniture, and modern pottery.

A fashionable look is also about context. A clawfoot bathtub will seem traditional in a room with floral prints and contemporary in an all-white context. Broadly speaking, "modern" is about clean unpatterned objects and simple lines—such as a plain white china jug—but at the moment it's also about the juxtaposition of old and new. Using utilitarian items— from wooden spoons to vintage shoes—as decoration is also very current.

what is *modern?*

The kitchen-living room on these and the following pages has both modern and traditional furniture in it, but it counts as a "contemporary" kitchen because of its simple use of color, and because most—although, crucially, not all—of its larger pieces have clean, modern lines. Combining modern and vintage items is very current, and prevents large open-plan spaces from seeming bland or too dated in a few years' time.

A fashionable kitchen ten or twenty years ago—indeed, this very kitchen—might have been fitted with natural pine units and rows of wall cupboards, while today's on-trend kitchen has open shelving and plain colors. Lucy Dickens, the artist owner of the house featured on these pages and through to page 85, was on a tight budget and was not able to remove the kitchen units that were already there, but, by painting them white, she updated them.

She also painted the floor white, creating a bright, contemporary effect, which was a perfect backdrop for one strong color: the red-orange of the dining chairs, wall clock, and some of the Le Creuset pans. The other traditional element is the Aga range cooker, but it fits in here because it is a classic design, which doesn't date.

Above left: An AGA is a classic range cooker that looks equally good in modern or traditional kitchens. For a contemporary look, keep colors and tiling plain and neutral in black, cream, or white. The best place to source similar pots and pans would be garage or car boot sales, as it's rare to find them on market stalls or in secondhand stores.

Above right: The dark orange chairs set the scene in an otherwise all-white kitchen. Even the flower pitcher is white, so the whole effect is very clean, fresh, and modern.

Mixing chain-store buys with flea-market finds is a recurrent theme in this book and it works very well in kitchens. International store IKEA—where this kitchen table was bought—is a great repository of modern design, but every town and city has its budget furniture store, and if you're buying budget, the simpler the better.

The flea-market element—the bright, modern orange chairs—is what defines this room. These came from a store specializing in old store fittings. There is no doubt that some of today's best bargains now come from industrial or commercial secondhand outlets, as is shown several times in this book. Finding such outlets isn't always obvious, but larger secondhand warehouses are more likely to have the space to take industrial quantities of furniture, and you can search online for secondhand office furniture, store fittings, catering equipment, or hotel furniture to find a list of used furniture companies. Look for secondhand dealers, house clearance, or similar in local directories and keep an eye out for local advertisements or billboards that are advertising used furniture. Secondhand business equipment companies don't only sell to other businesses and most are happy to sell off chairs or tables individually. As well as furniture, you can find some fantastic secondhand bargains from hotels in china, glass, and utensils, which are often priced by the box.

Above left: Lucy collects preserve jars because she likes the look of the various foods inside them. If your kitchen has too many wall units, you can take off a door to create a shelf effect.

Above center: Contemporary wooden bowls can be used for storage.

Above right: Update old-fashioned pine kitchen units with a pot of white paint. Flea-market finds include white china and old-fashioned kitchen scales.

Overleaf left: White units, floor, and walls create a modern backdrop for Lucy's vintage kitchen pots, pans, and utensils and her much-loved old Moroccan lampshade.

Overleaf right: Like the kitchen units, the pine shelf on the wall was transformed when Lucy painted it white. She collects old coffee pots, which are all used regularly.

kitchen-*living room*

The kitchen-living room is increasingly popular today, creating a modern, open-plan feel. Even where the shapes and sizes of the original rooms are retained, it's now quite common to make the doorway between them wider or to remove it altogether. This does, however, mean that both kitchen and living room need to have strong visual cohesion. A stainless steel kitchen and floral chintz living room, for example, would not flow well into each other!

Here, in Lucy Dickens' home, the all-white background of both rooms, the hints of red and orange, and the way the painted white floorboards are run through the two rooms establishes that key cohesion. There is a similar decorating philosophy in both of these rooms, too, which relies on one or two large key pieces and avoids clutter.

Above left: The only pictures in the room are propped on the mantelpiece. The warm red and orange theme is echoed in the lamp, the chest, and the little camel stool that Lucy bought from a Sikh upholsterer.

Above right: The mantelpiece is home to some papier-mâché elephants, brought back from an African market, and a collage by Jill Cogan.

Left: An antique desktop filing cabinet given to Lucy by her mother.

Right: The desk to the left of the door was found very cheaply in a storefitters' crowded basement. Always have look in the back of a store, or any side rooms, as that's often where bargains can be found. The French dresser is an antique, and the sofa, dating from the 1970s, was bought secondhand.

The controlled contemporary color palette works well. The dark orange chairs in the kitchen are echoed in bright, stripy orange pillows from the online furniture store Habitat. Other decorative elements pick up variations of the orange: a little button-box, a lampshade, a Knole sofa, and a vibrant painting. There is plenty of contrast in this room: antique and modern, textured and smooth, and a wide variety of things collected from all over the world, but it is a harmonious whole.

Simplicity is the key to looking modern. Here a large elaborate mirror and a dramatic rug make the maximum impact on the white background because there are no other pictures hanging on the walls. A mixed bag of armchairs and sofas, in various styles and from different eras, work together because there's no pattern—just texture—and they are all on a color spectrum that runs from brown to burnt-orange. Indeed, there is virtually no pattern at all in the room, except for the rugs and the pillows, and there are window shades instead of drapes or curtains.

Above left: The rug is upside down, as Lucy preferred the pattern on the underside. The armchair, a battered leather club chair, needed some restoration, but Lucy arranged for it to be restuffed and resprung without having to have it completely reupholstered and without losing its distressed charm.
Above right: Old-fashioned telephones—and their ring—have become newly fashionable.
Left: There is a vintage blanket on this secondhand French chair. Now that quilts have become so expensive, vintage blankets are the new clever buy for those wanting a folkloric feel. Look out for attractive colors, which often respond beautifully to dry cleaning. Wool and weaving are traditional to Wales, which is why Welsh blankets are considered to be of the highest quality.
Right: This room is an example of how context—the way you put things together—makes a room modern, even if your furnishings are antique or secondhand.

modern vintage *bedroom*

As in the kitchen, twenty years ago a "modern" bedroom would have had fitted glass-fronted wardrobes from wall to wall. Now a contemporary bedroom makes the most of unfitted storage wherever possible. Of course, it is necessary to have somewhere to keep clothes, but more is not always better. You need what you need, and only you know how much that is. Some people add a dressing room or walk-in closet to create a more relaxed and contemporary look with unfitted furniture, but that's not always necessary.

The all-white theme for walls and floors that runs through Lucy Dickens' house is carried upstairs to the bedroom. A Portuguese iron bedstead has been updated for the 21st century desire to have bigger beds—Lucy bought the bed from a company that extends traditional beds. Once again, there is just one big "statement" on the walls: a triptych of Lucy's own paintings. An antique Swedish armoire and an old Edwardian sea chest—painted white—that had been passed down through the family create useful storage. The Swedish armoire, however, has been left with its distressed look—the patina of age is often very attractive, so don't automatically paint a battered piece of furniture.

Left: Secondhand garden furniture is an excellent indoor purchase, too. Here, both the bedside table and the table seen through the door in the bathroom are garden tables, and the one by the bed has been repainted.

Above left: The top of the antique Swedish armoire is an ideal place to store vintage baskets.

Above center: A white lampshade, white vase, and white dressing table set make the old sea chest seem light and modern.

Above right: Old-fashioned dressing table sets don't have any value, but are very pretty. The little dressing table mirror is a good find, too. In the first half of the 20th century every woman had a three-sided mirror, so that she could check her profile and the back of her head, but they are rarely found new these days.

contemporary *bathroom*

How do a 1920s basin and a clawfooted bathtub end up in a chapter on modern flea market? As on the previous pages, it's all about context. "Modern" today means clean lines with one or two major statement pieces. Plumbing itself is pretty modern in the context of homes, as it didn't really hit the mass-market until the early twentieth century. Now bathrooms have bceome major lifestyle statements. The era of the "grand bathroom," however, was the 1920s, a time of vigorous advances in design, culture, and manufacturing. Art deco basins from the era are manufactured today, and still look contemporary.

Once again, the all-white theme allows the graceful lines of the basin and bathtub to make the main statement, which is why the room has a look that is fresh, uncluttered, and contemporary.

Left: The clawfoot bathtub is a reproduction, as is the 1920s basin, but the contemporary style is achieved through painting other elements of the room white. The mirror is an old French one.

Above left: This is a chest of old school lockers, bought long ago from a secondhand store. Lucy Dickens has painted them many times over.

Above right: The central panel of each door of this old German wardrobe was removed and replaced with glass. It was then painted white, updating a heavy piece of dark furniture with a light contemporary feel. Big pieces of "brown furniture" are relatively inexpensive today—look for pretty detail and a graceful overall shape.

Right: Classic perfume bottles are decorative in their own right.

natural *look*

The ground floor apartment on these and the following pages (up to page 95) belongs to Zoe Ellison, founder of i gigi, a fashion and lifestyle store in Brighton and Hove on Britain's south coast. Zoe's home and store have a similar ethos: a chic, modern look with a muted, earthy color palette that is also timeless. There's lots of recycling and "found" objects, a clever use of unexpected materials or items, and a very contemporary interpretation of vintage style.

Zoe's kitchen is made of reclaimed oak floorboards and inexpensive birch ply, which she painted this stylish shade of gray-blue. She had it made by a carpenter

Above left: The Danish "wishbone" chair is on the left, and on the right is a country classic style known as a Windsor chair. Variations can be found all over the world.

Above right: Salt-glaze stoneware storage jars used to be common in every home. Now there are but a few companies still making traditional salt-glaze stoneware. However, there are lots still available—indeed, i gigi sell them—and they are increasingly collectable.

Left: Zoe bought a pair of reclaimed Indian pillars for her kitchen in Britain.

friend, which gave her the option of getting exactly what she wanted—reclaimed oak shelving and drawers, plus little touches, such as a pull-out spice drawer. The wall shelving is also made from reclaimed oak floorboards, as is the floor. "I wanted the wider oak floorboards," she said, "because wider boards add a sense of space." In fact, most of the kitchen is reclaimed or recycled, including the old-fashioned radiators, which she had shot-blasted to remove the paint and flushed through inside. It's not cheap to restore old radiators, but they give out a very solid warmth—the sturdy iron design retains heat well, so they are not expensive to run once you've renovated them.

The chairs are 1950s classics: the "wishbone chair" on the left was designed by Hans J Wegner, one of Denmark's most successful and award-winning 20th-century designers. Made by Carl Hansen & Son, it is still being manufactured, but it was popular enough worldwide for there to be thousands available on the secondhand market.

You don't have to restrict your flea-market finds to things that are small enough to take home in the car. One of the most striking elements of Zoe's kitchen is a pair of Indian pillars, which she bought ten years ago. She bought them from a man who specialized in bringing architectural reclamation over from India, so she didn't need to arrange shipping, but it is possible to do this if necessary.

Above left: Reclaimed oak floorboards as shelving, on which Zoe displays her collections of vintage children's shoes (she always buys white ones), as well as a Buddha, shells, bark, and stones with lichen on them.

Above right: Zoe keeps fresh food in a variety of bowls found in secondhand stores and on market stalls. She then stacks the bowls on a traditional pot stand, saving space.

Overleaf left: The gray kitchen units were handmade of birch ply, then painted. An old Hungarian trough holds sink paraphernalia.

Overleaf right: Think about shape, texture, and color when considering what to hang on your walls. Who would have thought that three dried sunflower heads, seen on the wall above the carved table, would fit in so well next to carved horses' heads from India? The equally weathered and textured Turkish pot has been converted into the perfect lamp for this collection of found and bought objects.

texture *and tone*

Zoe's living room continues with the muted, chic look. One of i gigi's specialties is reupholstering secondhand furniture with the vintage linens that the store has sourced from countries such as Hungary. The texture of such fabrics has integrity and elegance, as you can see from the furniture here. The armchair, for example, is reupholstered in antique linen. It is a Howard chair—Howard being the foremost British makers of upholstery in the 19th century, and their chair shapes have become classics. The cushions are made from small pieces of silk or velvet that Zoe has collected over the years.

Zoe also wanted the look of old furniture, but the practicality of modern storage, so she bought two single old doors and fitted them to new cabinets, "because antique cupboards often aren't very practical." It is through this method of mixing and matching that you can bring together an old style and modern practicality.

It's worth thinking about how you can use interesting items to add character to a room. For example, objects you find on your travels work well—here an African drum makes an original coffee table, and an old Indian refrigerator, in the fireplace, has been turned into a little cupboard. Similarly, you can make use of items with personal significance to inspire you. A painting of a woman over the fireplace, in the atmospheric charcoal and earth tones that define the rest of the apartment, was painted by Zoe's father, Peter Ellison; obviously, they both have a similar eye.

Left: The mirror came from Zoe's mother. Zoe stripped the paint off, right down to the wood. She's done the same with the little kitchen chair to the right of the fireplace. The trend for stripping in the 1970s created a vast stockpile of orange pine, but paler woods look elegant when they're taken back to the grain.
Above right: Zoe bought two attractive old doors and put them on the front of modern cupboards to maximize storage. The lampshade has been made out of antique linen.
Right: Cushions made from scraps of luxurious fabrics.
Far right: Zoe made the chandelier herself out of seashells, on a structure almost like a child's hanging mobile.

passing *through*

Hallways may be places where people only pass through, but if you've got a flea-market habit, then you'll need every inch of wall for displays.

This is the hallway in Zoe's apartment, and she uses it to display a huge range of photographs of her family and friends. She collects old frames, so they're all different shapes, sizes, and styles. However, she paints those that aren't black already, so that all the frames are one color once hung up on the wall. She gives the display even more unity by having any color photos converted into black and white.

This hallway could have looked cluttered—not only is there a huge display of photographs, but it also houses coat hooks, an old-fashioned radiator, and a place to hang a poncho. However, it retains its light, airy feel with some clever tricks. First, the woodwork and the walls are the same color, opening the space out. If you want a room to feel as wide as possible, try not to interrupt sight lines. Second, the photographs are on one wall, leaving the other almost clear. Photos on both sides would have closed in the space.

Left: The walls are packed tightly with an ever-changing collection of photographs of family and friends in frames collected at markets, sales, and thrift or charity stores.
Above left: These two lampshades are made from shell, which has been etched, and hung underneath ceiling spotlights, so that when the lights are on, the pattern shines through. If you have a long, narrow hall, hanging a row of two or more chandeliers or lights is more effective than a single one dangling in the space.
Above right: Have colored photographs printed in black-and-white for maximum effect in a grouping.

Always remember life is short.
Forgive quickly, kiss slowly!
Laugh in love uncontrollably
And never regret anything that

new *romantic*

Once again, it is texture and soft, earthy neutrals that create the atmosphere in this romantic bedroom. The old French bed has been stripped back to the wood and reupholstered in antique linen, and the duvet cover is also made of antique linen. Zoe finds it difficult to find really attractive good-quality duvet covers and bed linen at an affordable price, so she makes her own out of the antique fabric they import for the store. Anyone who is frustrated by the quality/price ratio of today's duvet covers could do the same with any good fabric they like, although it is important to check that it is machine washable. You need to be able to sew only a straight line to make the covers, so even beginners could have a go.

Zoe's use of storage is innovative, because she has combined decorative appeal and function in a number of different ways. Conventionally, there is an old-fashioned wardrobe (on top of which are stored bags and hats). Then, in the fireplace gap, there is a vintage trunk, used for keeping clothes, while the mannequin beside it is a useful repository for necklaces and hats. More jewelry is kept in a store jewelry display cabinet, from a store that she spotted when it was closing down and getting rid of its fittings. She's added extra rails inside for earrings. And finally, two old French apple-picking ladders, brought back from France on Eurostar, are used for hanging clothes, boots, and bags.

Left: The furniture was all found in markets, auctions, and thrift or charity stores. An old French bed, with a Victorian milking stool as a space-saving bedside table, is furnished with Zoe's handmade duvet covers, made from antique linen. The poem on the wall was sent to her by a friend, so Zoe photographed it and projected the transparency onto the wall. She then copied out the lettering herself.

Above left: Above this French farmhouse chair is a store display cabinet, which was bought from a jewelry store that was closing down.

Above right: A battered antique mirror, a Victorian dummy used for jewelry and hats, and a vintage trunk for clothes. All are available from secondhand stores, auctions, and markets, although vintage trunks are now becoming quite expensive.

Above left: These little dishes are called Wonki Ware, and come from South Africa.

Above: The settle came from a market and Alex stripped it of its paint. Beneath it are old apple boxes, which make useful storage. Alex drilled holes in the breadboards so that she could hang them up. They're collected over the years from various markets.

Above right: The wall clock is a reproduction railway clock, stocked by i gigi.

Above far right: The cushion is made from antique linen.

recycled *kitchen*

The apartment on these pages, up to pages 105, belongs to Alex Legendre, Zoe's partner in i gigi, the menswear, womenswear, and lifestyle store. It's on the top two floors of a Regency terrace near the store.

Alex's kitchen, like Zoe's, is handmade out of reclaimed wood, and is equipped with things she's picked up over the years. All Alex's family are involved in antiques, markets, or fairs, so she's grown up with this ethos.

As in many city kitchens there's not much room for more than a single run of units, plus a few other pieces of furniture. Here, that run of units is made up of a mishmash of reclaimed pieces of wood from a local salvage yard, which "cost virtually nothing." The work surface is made from solid oak floorboards. Extra-high wall

cupboards leave plenty of space for the kitchen countertop and don't intrude into the room too much. The plain white tiles are in a classic "railway" brick pattern, and Alex's collection of kitchenalia picks up on both the wood and the white themes.

What makes Alex's style—like Zoe's—so modern is her contemporary and individualistic use of shape and texture rather than color in her decorating. She doesn't hang pictures on the walls, preferring to decorate with interesting objects or practical items that are of use. Within this clever, disciplined framework, she is a magpie, and warns other would-be collectors that "once you start, you can't stop. Both Zoe's and my home are an extension of the store. We're constantly evolving and everything's a work in progress, depending on what we're interested in at the time."

Overleaf left: The kitchen—both the units and the work surface—is made with reclaimed wood. Note how the wall cupboards are positioned high up, so that they don't intrude into the working space.

Overleaf right: The dresser houses Zoe's collection of jars, pitchers, bowls, and spoons. The advantage of collecting spoons (and the molds cast for them—see the center of the second shelf down) is that "they're easy to take home when you find them," she says. "And each one has its story."

dramatic *statements*

One strong contemporary direction is to have a neutral backdrop, then just one or two major statement pieces, which can be quite elaborate. The statement piece in this room is the early 19th-century Italian lead crystal chandelier, bought from an antique store. Beautiful chandeliers, such as this one, can be either wired up or used with candles. If they are wired up, make sure that you have them on dimmers, as a low overhead light is more comfortable than a bright one. And if they have candles, try to use good-quality non-drip candles.

The key to this hall-dining room comes from the natural-plaster wall treatment. Alex and Zoe also run a decorating advice service, and one of their specialities is this pale plaster. Unlike ordinary plaster, which has a pink tinge, this raw white plaster is almost creamy, and they apply it with a view to leave it unpainted, creating a calm backdrop.

Against this is set the natural textures of linen, wood, and bone. Instead of having pictures on the walls, she prefers to display the things she's collected, with quirky items like antlers on the wall, and little statuettes or pieces of coral displayed under Victorian-style glass domes. The Victorians first used glass domes to protect clocks from dust, but they were also great collectors and soon began to use them to protect stuffed animals and other treasures. As well as being easier to dust than, say, an intricate piece of coral, the domes also give an item a little extra impact on the shelf.

With five doors opening onto this room, there isn't space for tables and lamps, so extra lighting comes from attractive wall lights. Wall lights are coming back, having fallen out of favor in the early 1990s. They are practical and give a flattering light.

Above far left: The area at the top of the stairs is a hallway-cum-dining room, with other rooms leading off it. The sofa has been reupholstered in vintage linen and the table is made out of reclaimed oak.

Above left: A set of antlers and a shelf of interesting shapes and textures in place of pictures. A shelf is a good way to show off quirky collections that you've picked up at flea markets or secondhand stores, and it doesn't have to be part of a bookcase. Simply think of it as you would a painting.

Above: A piece of coral, statuettes under glass domes, and vintage shoes, with a 17th-century Italian mirror.

Right: An early English fruitwood chair.

Far right: French 1920s wall lights.

flea market *modern*

shaker-style *simplicity*

Finding the right bathroom furniture can be difficult, and washstands seem to be either available in only a few designs or very expensive. Converting a piece of furniture, such as a table or a chest, is a good option.

The key place to start is to measure your space and the height at which you need the washstand to be. Having a bowl on top is very current, and it also makes the height issue easier. If you were to sink a basin into this Victorian desk, it would probably be too low for comfortable use. This way, it sits on top, with the plumbing cut through the center, and a block behind to raise up the faucets or taps.

The simple Shaker-style peg rail and shelf above is ideal for storing towels, and you can acquire a shaving or makeup mirror from most garage or car boot sales.

Above left: Don't forget that plumbing will need to be raised up if the basin sits on top of a washstand.

Above right: A Shaker-style chair echoes the shelf and pegboard.

Left: Shoe trees are a good example of the new collectables: beautiful utilitarian everyday objects that were once made in large quantities.

Right: Antique washstands, with their marble or tiled tops, have now become quite expensive and difficult to find in antique stores. But you can still pick up a pine Victorian desk quite cheaply, as seen here converted into a washstand. Other items that could also be converted include small chests of drawers and tables, but check measurements carefully.

the new *neutrals*

Decorating with naturals and neutrals has always been stylish. Ten years ago, this meant beige, cream, and natural wood, but that now looks bland and outdated. This bedroom, belonging to Alex's teenage daughter, is a great example of how decorating with neutrals has been updated and has edge—using cream, black, and polished wood.

It's an elegant version of the stereotypical black-walled teenage room. One whole wall is painted with blackboard paint, so she can write or draw on it as she likes. "It's a twist on graffiti," says Alex, "and was inspired by a little black chest of drawers I bought that had lots of things scrawled or painted on it." The rest of the walls have been left as raw plaster, in a soft creamy-pink color with a slightly textured finish.

The walls are bare of paintings. Mizzy's name is spelt out in a mix of different antique gold letters picked up over time, and some antlers, above the grouping of black-and-white family photographs, add a Gothic touch. Empty, used scent bottles create another inexpensive and attractive collection. A one-off dining chair in beautifully polished wood accompanies an old office desk. While sets of chairs are expensive, it's easy to pick up good-quality antique chairs as one-offs—they're often cheaper than buying new!

Battered furniture works well for teenagers, because a bit more wear doesn't matter. As well as the distressed chest of drawers, there's a comfortable but stylish leather armchair.

Left: The oversized mirror is perched on two old wooden crates, turned sideways. A panel of Indian fabric has been used to make a window shade.

Above: The black theme is emphasized by the black-framed family photographs, the antlers, and the black typewriter. Using black as a highlight color is a trick interior decorators sometimes use to prevent a room looking too bland—which is not an issue here, but it is still very effective.

Right: Mannequins can be bought from secondhand storefitters, and are both decorative and a useful place to hang things. Mirrors like this are relatively easy to find in markets and sales. If they still have their original silvered glass, don't replace it as you will make the mirror look too new and may destroy its value.

tricks *of the trade*

The home on these pages and up to page 117 belongs to interiors stylist Melanie Molesworth, whose work can be found in a number of top interiors magazines. She scours yard sales and car boot fairs, online auctions, secondhand stores, thrift and charity stores, and markets, not only for bargains, but also for unusual items to use in her work. And she collects, too—for example, she specializes in Cathrineholm, the enamelware of the mid-century modern Norwegian designer Grete Prytz Kittelsen, seen here displayed in the aubergine-painted dresser.

Cathrineholm enamelware is a good example of an online auction collectable. The designs aren't being manufactured anymore, so they're sold only individually. Not everyone gets the spelling right, even when they're selling them, so you're advised to try several spellings when you're searching. Cathrineholm, as one word, is the correct spelling for the enamelware, but you may also find it listed under "Catherine Holme" (with an "e" in Cathrine or Holm), "Cathrine Home," or "Catherinehome." Try every variation of an item you want to buy, because a misspelling may mean fewer rival bidders! Do this with descriptions, too, when you're searching—for example, if you're looking for Welsh blankets, try "vintage blankets," "Welsh blankets," and so on. Some searches bring up too many results and others too few, but you'll soon work it out.

Left: Some people love blue but find it difficult to decorate with because it can look cold on walls. Melanie instead used this color elsewhere—she revitalized old kitchen units by painting them blue, and added a blue-gray tablecloth to match, which works very well, particularly with the stainless steel lamps above the table.

Above left: Melanie always keeps an eye out for little vases, glass, and china to use on the shoots she styles.

Above center: Cathrineholm enamelware from the 1950s, which Melanie has collected over the years using eBay.

Above right: Melanie had the dresser painted an unusual purple color, making it an effective backdrop for display. Here there are books and collected enamelware, china, and glass.

Melanie also searches online auctions by putting general headings into the search engine, such as "modernist," and then filters the search for "home and garden." You could do the same with "vintage," "antique," or "retro." She generally restricts herself to items for which bids are ending within the next 48 hours. This way, you have less to trawl through. Use a search engine, such as Google, to find out more about the product you are collecting: Grete Prytz Kittelsen, for example, was known as the "Queen of Scandinavian Design" and she won many awards in the 1950s. There are usually fan pages and groups to be found, too. All this information means you can quickly learn what sorts of prices are being paid for your collectables, and when you've got a bargain.

Other online auction buying tips include making sure that you know what you're bidding on. Occasionally, you may think you are bidding on an object, but you're actually only bidding on a link to a sales site for it (this is a more common scam when selling new electronics rather than secondhand items), so always read the

Above left: Clever ways with family photographs. Some are pinned onto a piece of reclaimed wood that was once used as a bed headboard. The others are framed. Melanie's advice is to keep the frames fairly similar and use wide white or cream mounts around each photo within the frame to give the image plenty of space. It's a way of making family photographs into works of art.

Above: Chairs like this were often used in restaurants, so there are lots around and they are hardwearing.

description to the end before bidding. If you want to find out what price you might expect to pay for something, search for recently completed sales on similar items—this is very helpful. And, finally, you can register a "favorites" search on eBay, so that when sellers list something you want to hear about, such as Cathrineholm enamelware, you'll receive an email with details of the new sale.

Meanwhile, Melanie's sunny, stylish family home is full of finds that she's picked up in the course of her work. The kitchen table, as seen on the previous page, came from a shoot: "I was photographing a couple who were downsizing, and they wanted to sell their kitchen table because it was going to be too big for their new house. So I bought it." Similarly, the weathered wood that now holds an array of family photographs was a piece of reclaimed wood, which was bought to be a bedhead on a photography shoot. Most of the chairs, china, glass, and storage canisters are secondhand-store or flea-market buys, and her kitchen scales are old postal service scales. The whole effect is elegant, relaxed, and stylish.

Above left: Melanie has lots of china and glass, picked up from markets, fairs, and thrift stores, much of which she uses in her work. She usually displays them in groups of similar items, such as all the white china pieces, or all the glasses of a particular type.

Above right: Vintage kitchenalia is a new collectable area. Storage tins and jars, in particular, can be picked up cheaply. They were once made in huge quantities for every home in the land when coffee, tea, flour, and sugar were sold loose in grocery stores.

simple *living*

Melanie Molesworth's living room has the pared-down style currently in fashion, but much of the furniture is either secondhand or she has owned it for a long time, showing that you don't have to buy brand new furniture to look contemporary. The large sofa came from British homeware store Heal's many years ago (Heal's is a good name to look for when identifying modern furniture in auctions or secondhand stores). When its arms showed signs of wear, Melanie's mother made arm covers for it from scraps of Osborne and Little fabric.

There's everything you need in the room—lights, a side table, comfortable seating—but nothing unnecessary. The side table is in fact a little stool, taking up hardly any space, but offering the perfect resting place for a cup of coffee or a book. Color and art are spare but effective, such as a tiny photograph taken by her son, and purple linen panels used as curtains. Blues and purples are still a predominant highlight color, but they are lightly used.

Above left: Simply furnished with plain walls and floor, this living room allows the sofa and a few market finds—bentwood chairs, an old Victorian stool, and Bakelite lamps—to add character. Such restraint creates a spacious feel. The two bentwood chairs are almost, but not quite, identical. They've been painted with historic paint colors.

Above right: Melanie collects medicine bottles and often uses them as vases.

Right: The soft blue in the alcove in the hall echoes the blue in the Victorian floor tiles. The rest of the hall walls are white—the contrast makes an attractive feature.

This is the other end of Melanie Molesworth's living room, and here the background is just as simple, but the accent colors are black and lime green. Acid greens and yellows like these are very mid-century modern, with a strong flavor of the 1950s and 1960s, so they have come back into fashion with the increasing interest in this era.

The striking office chair was one of Melanie's eBay bargains—it cost less than $40 (£30), and the dresser behind it was also a clever buy. She had a pine dresser, which she wanted to replace, so when she saw this dresser in a secondhand store, she asked the store-keeper if he would be interested in part-exchange. Many secondhand or antique stores do this quite often, if your piece of furniture is in their style, as it's always good to keep turning stock over. She's lined the back of it with a few scraps of a luxurious wallpaper, which makes a great backdrop for her collection of white china, pewter, and silver.

Left: The principle of accent color—that is, small splashes of a vibrant or contrasting color—is well established in interior decorating. Here there is also accent pattern—an essentially plain room with touches of pattern in the lampshade and the dresser lining. It's a very modern look.

Above left: An office chair, instead of an armchair, looks elegant and saves space.

Above right: The top shelf of the dresser houses some of Melanie's pewter collection. Pewter is seen by some as silver's "poor relation," but is an ancient tin alloy. Made in large quantities since Medieval times, older pewter has often been melted and reused, so most collectable pieces are now fewer than a hundred years old.

Right: Christmas decorations are great collectables, too, and can be used as ornaments all year round. Look out for specialist Christmas fairs.

original *features*

Melanie Molesworth has chosen a streamlined and uncluttered look for her hall, and a striking graphic treatment for the stairs. The house still had its original hall tiles in good condition, and they're attractive and easy to keep clean. Instead of covering them with carpet or wooden flooring, she decided to keep them without going ultra-Victorian in feel for the rest of the decoration.

Britain's Victorian era officially dated from 1819 to 1901, the years of Queen Victoria's reign. However "Victorian" has come to stand for mid-to-late 19th-century architectural fashion worldwide, as this time was when Britain was internationally influential. By the late 20th century, Victorian houses all over the world had become run down and had begun to be renovated. There was an initial instinct to destroy or cover up any worn down original features. Thousands of houses were "modernized," with their ceiling coving, fireplaces, doors, and other period features taken out. Now modernizing is very different. Original features—whether they're a 1950s fitted kitchen or an 1850s fireplace—are celebrated, even if they're quite battered or not what you would have chosen in the first place. They give a house a sense of belonging.

Melanie also kept the Victorian stair rail and banisters. At one stage these were boxed in or even replaced, but now people appreciate that you can make something look modern with a coat of paint, which is cheap, easy, and can always be removed.

Above left: The stairs are painted with dark navy blue where the stair runner would have been.
Above right: Chests of drawers like this are reliably found on the secondhand market—here, painted white, it looks elegant and up-to-date.
Right: The two rusted ceiling tiles were bought from a salvage yard in Canada. One of the vases is an empty French wine carafe and the other is from Melanie's collection of medicinal glassware.
Overleaf left: The two green-and-black chairs were part of a set of three, bought very cheaply from eBay. The cabinets above were made by her husband and the desk is a modified IKEA desk. Everything—the desk, lamp, floors, and walls—is in one color for a fresh, modern style.
Overleaf right: Melanie's collection of shoe trees. Made from natural materials, hundreds of thousands of them were produced, even though many were made by hand. Look for the beauty in everyday items when considering what to collect.

Chapter 5

collectors'
flea market

Collecting makes flea-market shopping fun. You develop "an eye" and soon learn to spot your favorites in a pile of clutter. And there's always something very attractive about displaying a group of similar items: blue-and-white china, teapots, vintage toys or packaging, clocks, instruments, signs, royal memorabilia, menus, wooden shoe trees... the list is infinite. All that is required is enthusiasm, time, and a small amount of money.

Of course some collectors' items are immensely valuable, but most collections have little or no intrinsic value. Others suddenly become fashionable and prices rise, like vintage cigarette cards or 1950s toy cars. Some people collect machinery, such as old lawn mowers or typewriters, while others look for beauty. Forget about investment. Go for things you love, and find out as much as you can about them.

the collectors' *kitchen*

The rooms on these pages and through to page 127 belong to restaurateur-cum-rock photographer Kerstin Rodgers. Kerstin, otherwise known as MsMarmitelover, runs The Underground Restaurant, a supper club in London, and she also cooks for rock festivals. She spent many years living in Paris, where she honed her French style and her love of food. She collects china, glass, and kitchenalia, because The Underground Supper Club is a pop-up restaurant that she runs from her own living room. Once a week, the room is transformed into a home restaurant. Guests bring their own wine and share tables with each other. Kerstin is also the author of a cookery book, *Supper Club: Recipes and Notes from the Underground Restaurant*, and runs links to other supper clubs.

Kerstin says that she has always loved kitchens, preferring to visit the kitchen when she's going round stately homes or public attractions, such as Monet's house. Her collecting theme starts with blue-and-white china, which she gets from garage and car boot sales, thrift and charity stores, *brocantes* and *dépôt-ventes* in France (antique and secondhand stores), or what the French call *vide greniers*—attic

Above left: Vintage colanders are getting popular, and sometimes seem to have surprisingly high prices, but you can still pick up reasonably priced examples if you keep an eye out.

Above: Everything is easily to hand on open shelves, as Kerstin is sometimes cooking for up to thirty people.

Above right: A vintage-style clock, which is actually from IKEA.

Above right center: The scalloped edges for the shelves were bought from a DIY chain store.

Above far right: Kerstin cooks with pans bought from fairs and flea markets, as old-fashioned iron and copper conduct heat well and are sturdy.

sales. If you're on vacation in France, she says, look out for advertisements for *vide greniers* or *dépôt-ventes*, because these are where you will find the real secondhand bargains.

Hotel crockery and glassware is another of her collecting enthusiasms, because it is sturdy, practical, and attractive. Drinking glasses made for hotels and restaurants don't shatter easily, and they're cheaper than domestic glass. "Part of the inspiration for the restaurant is the memory of eating in formal rural French hotels," she says, "where the food is simple but beautifully presented and delicious." She even makes her own French jam, called Mauvaise Maman.

Kerstin, like many successful flea-market shoppers, keeps an eye out for a bargain at all times. She drives a van, rather than a car, so she's always ready to pick up anything that attracts her interest and take it home—for example, she found the dresser in her kitchen (on page 124) literally standing on the street in Paris. "Everything has memories," she says.

Overleaf left: Many of the shelves have been cut down from wooden bedheads. "Never throw bits of wood away," says Kerstin. The higher shelves show off the better-quality, more ornamental plates, while the china on the lower shelves is crockery that is always in use.

Overleaf right: There are two wrought iron shelves in Kerstin's kitchen. One came from a market in France and the other was bought on the internet. The glass mainly came from secondhand stores—Kerstin looks out for glasses made by La Rochère, the oldest glassware company in France (still trading), because their designs are so attractive. The *chemin du bonheur* ("the way to happiness") sign came from a market.

vintage
kitchenalia

All Kerstin's collections are used in her home restaurant. Nothing has cost too much, so a few breakages don't really matter. Odd plates and mugs cost very little individually, but look good together, and now that she's so associated with blue-and-white china, friends often give her pieces, too, as presents. When buying, she sets herself a budget of paying, say, no more than $1.50 (£1) for an individual plate, and mixes vintage finds with modern chain-store buys.

Kerstin's other collections include old copper and cast-iron pans. She cooks with these. "A properly seasoned cast-iron pan is genuinely nonstick," she says, "but you need to be careful that the lining for copper pans isn't too worn, because it can make food taste metallic."

She also collects enamelware, which can go in the fridge and the oven and is unbreakable. Kerstin uses enamel plates for picnics instead of paper plates—they're so much more stylish, and don't get thrown away at the end. Finally, bowls and colanders are used for storage as well as for draining. The circulating air makes a vintage colander an excellent fruit bowl.

Left: Kerstin repainted the inside of this dresser, which she found in Paris, but will never cover up its original distressed laundry-blue color on the outside. She also added shelves, as well as strips of wood so that plates could balance safely at the back.

Above right: This is a garden table, covered with a tablecloth—Kerstin also collects linen—and set with blue-and-white china. The eggcups were a present. Once people know what you collect, they'll often spot things for you. The benches are garden furniture, too.

Right: An old Christmas decoration.

Far right: A hotelware carafe.

outside *inside*

Kerstin's home is an apartment in London, so she has little space to store furniture. But when the Underground Supper Club is open, she has to seat lots of people. The solution is garden furniture, which she can store outside.

Anyone who is short of space can maximize their flexibility by using garden furniture inside, but be careful of the effect of sharp metal feet on some floors. Garden furniture is also a particularly good flea-market find, as there has been an explosion of styles over the past few decades, much of which you can now pick up in secondhand stores or in garage or car boot sales.

The principles are the same as with other collections: go for what you like and forget about value. You don't necessarily need to paint or restore it—in fact, the distressed look is attractive—but be aware that if metal has started to rust, it will continue. If you're painting a metal chair, sand down the patches of rust, apply a metal primer, and then continue with any outdoor paint.

Left: The chairs are garden chairs, and were a present. The photographs on the walls are by Kerstin Rodgers herself.

Above top left: Kerstin found the little bentwood chair on the street.

Above top center: Jars and bottles are cheap and easy to collect, and they are great in groups with one or two flowers in each.

Above left: The alphabet hooks were bought from home store Anthropologie and spell out the word "underground."

Above right: The menu is written on the mirror. Kerstin also collects small mirrors and uses them decoratively.

a magpie *eye*

The cornucopia of collections on these pages through to page 133 are packed into the home of illustrator Mark Hearld. His work is based on observing the natural world, in the tradition of artists such as Edward Bawden and Eric Ravilious. In 2009 he organized an exhibition in Scarborough that combined traditional folk art and the work of contemporary artists working in popular art, which was appropriately called The Magpie Eye. It is this mix of folk and contemporary art that informs his collections.

He's also a printmaker and collagemaker, and has designed textiles, china, and illustrated children's books. His main specialty collecting areas are old toys, ceramics, and textiles. Mark constantly searches in secondhand stores and at fairs, and has established certain specific things to look out for—for example, Rye Pottery spongeware and English Delft tin-glazed lusterware mugs.

Above left: Mark's own pottery is mixed with lusterware mugs, mainly from markets and fairs, a 20th-century coffee set, and other china.

Above right: The picture above the boots is by Mark and was commissioned by the Curwen Press to celebrate fifty years in business.

Left: Packaging is also one of Mark's collections—anything with a strong, graphic style and often featuring one of his favorite themes, birds.

Right: Mark says that this dresser may appear to contain random items, but it's actually in a strict order. It focuses on highly decorative spotted and colored china and includes studio pottery, mugs by RAMP Ceramics and David Garland, a 1934 coffee service designed by English artist Graham Sutherland, and a pottery hen, which was an Emma Bridgewater blank decorated by Mark himself.

crowding *up*

"Crowding up" is an old collectors' trick, and is also seen in this book on page 40, where it makes the most of a display of family pictures. Here, in Mark Hearld's home, every spare inch of wall is used. "The effect is more than just the sum of its parts," says Mark. He likes to use visual repetition in his displays—it might look as if collections have been randomly flung together, but this "crowding up" works because there are several repeating themes. The major themes are perhaps the birds and the stuffed animals, which appear in paintings, as sculptures, on textiles, and even as taxidermy.

Other themes include old signs and packaging, repeated throughout, and there is very little abstract art. Most work is figurative or a representation of nature, however stylized. Arrows, flags, signs, and sign-writing all continue the graphic theme. Portraits are realistic, sculptures are of animals, and even textiles or china often depict realistic scenes. Keeping to a few themes means that the whole display works together.

Even where patterns are found—mainly on china and textiles—they have a charming folksy quality with lots of repetition. Mark is part of a large artistic community so many of the pictures on his wall are by friends, but this particular contemporary folk style can be found on greetings cards, prints, and packaging, so you don't have to be an artist yourself, or to know artists, to be able to afford to build a similar collection.

Left: The pigeonhole shelves came from an antique dealer who knew Mark and put them aside for him. On the sofa, there is a horse blanket, plus pillows and cushions designed by Mark himself. Underneath is a large drawer used for storage. Some of the paintings were created by Mark for the Tate art museum store in London.

barter *and swap*

Many collectors tune into the power of swapping, and Mark, who knows lots of other artists, often exchanges one picture for another. It's perhaps a little difficult to establish the exact financial value in barter, but if there's something you want, and the other person wants something of yours, then money is less important. Mark has even exchanged very dissimilar things: a plan chest for a painting, for example, or a couple of paintings for a suit.

Mark says that the key to barter is being sure that the other person really wants something of yours or that there is genuine mutual admiration of each other's collections or work. The initial approach might be quite lighthearted, with a throwaway remark such as, "I'd always be interested in swapping that with you, if you're ever thinking of getting rid of it." Once you're known as a swapper, people will often come up with their own suggestions.

Left: The display box on the wall is an old noticeboard, which was being thrown away. Mark keeps ephemera to do with his work inside it—sketches, letters, and photographs, plus some market and fair finds. The pictures below are done by a textile artist friend, Sue Dennis.

Above left: Mark commissioned a signwriter to do the boards on the wall: They are the names of artists he admires.

Above right: The bird theme continues in the bedroom—above the door is a linocut by Mark Hearld called "Minsters and Magpies," and above the scarves is a rag rug by Louisa Creed.

Right: The pelican was one of a collection of wooden cutout toys Mark found in a flea market in Berlin. He repaired the beak, but one day it fell off again and was accidentally vacuumed up.

Chapter 6

flea market
outside

By the time you've decorated your house, there often isn't a large budget left over for the garden. However, outside space is increasingly important as a place to relax and entertain friends. The answer is the flea market: the secondhand, thrift and charity stores, the internet, and architectural salvage yards. You can even buy an unusual garden room secondhand. Our outside hideaways include a converted fishing trawler and an old rail freight wagon, as well as a handmade shed.

Some vintage garden furniture fetches surprisingly high prices, as good furniture lasts longer. Get a feel for what's on offer by visiting expensive garden and florists' stores to see what they're charging, then look for similar items when they come up secondhand.

flea market *afloat*

This converted fishing trawler has been done up by double-bass player Rutledge Turnlund. He has carried out almost all the renovation himself—except the specialist work, such as plumbing and electrics—and virtually everything in the boat is secondhand, usually from a market or fair. The boat was built in Scotland in 1952 for catching sprat, a small oily fish. Now its pilothouse, where the steering wheel was located, is a kitchen, and its hold, where the sprat would have been stored, is a cozy sitting room.

He made the kitchen cabinets himself from doors he already owned, miscellaneous pieces of wood, and a butler's sink he bought from an online auction. Rutledge had some brass faucets (taps), which he swapped with a plumber to get these old-fashioned nickel-plated ones. The countertop was cut from a piece of oak about to be thrown out from a kitchen that was being refurbished. All the kitchen equipment comes from markets.

Above left: The silver column is the chimney from a large Rayburn stove in the cabin below. It helps to heat the boat in winter. The handles on the cabinets, made by Rutledge, himself are old coat hooks.

Above right: Rutledge collects gauges, which he picks up very cheaply. The lamp is an old mechanical inspection lamp (as used by professional garages) and was bought at a fair.

Left: The kettle, found at a fair, is used on a camping stove.

Right: The pilothouse kitchen. Rutledge's children found the small mirrored first-aid cabinet at a scrapheap, and the map was a present from his mother, who had come across it at a market. The knife rack came from a secondhand store and the draining board cost 75 cents (50 pence) from a car boot sale, but all electrical fittings are new, and painted over.

cabin *fever*

This is the hold where the sprat was stored until the trawler returned to port and could send its haul to market. The ceiling would have been open to the sky, so that when the fish-filled nets were pulled on board, the sprats would have been tipped straight into the hold. When the trawler was decommissioned in the 1970s, a roof was put on the hold, and the benches you see here were fitted in the style of the bunk in the cabin.

Rutledge bought the solid-fuel Rayburn stove from eBay, and had it lowered in. This heats the boat and provides an oven for stews and roasts. He found the kitchen table on the top of a bonfire and rescued it (before the fire was lit!). It was covered in lino, which he scraped off with a knife, and then he added two chairs that came from a fair.

Left: The wood for the solid-fuel Rayburn stove is kept in a giant bread bin, which was bought at a fair, as was the engineer's lamp hanging from the ceiling. The lamp had to be rewired.

Above left: Rutledge added the word "engine" to the door using some stencils he found at a fair, and got the "bar open" sign from Canada through an online auction. He had it rewired so that it functions as a useful light.

Above right: The pillows and cushions were made from attic curtains, and the lamp is an old paraffin railway lamp. It still works.

Right: The picture was painted by Rutledge's daughter, aged ten. The clock came from eBay and the coffee pot and storage canisters were from a market.

marine
hideaway

This bunk was original to the boat and once slept four sprat fisherman, who would have taken it in turns to sleep two on-duty and two off-duty while they were at sea. A boat needs constant renovation, as it is always under attack from both sea water and rain, so there are inevitably patches of new paint where there have been repairs.

Canal boats and houseboats have long been used as weekend hideaways, but it's easy to overlook the more practical boats. Yet they are very good purchases—and this trawler is shorter than most houseboats, so attracts lower mooring charges in the harbor. With a contracting fishing industry, there should be some good bargains available, but be realistic about the time, effort, and money it can take to repair and maintain a boat.

Furnishing a boat doesn't mean you have to keep to boatone doesn't go to sea, there's no need to worry about screwing everything down or having water-resistant sleeping bags. The space between the ribs of the boat makes great shelving for storage—although the boat is quite cold in winter, so you might want to also consider increasing the insulation.

Left: The former fishermen's bunk is now repainted in soft, historic gray, with the ribs of the boat used as bookshelves. It does get very cold on winter nights, so a pile of quilts and extra bedding is a good idea.

Right: Flowers have been picked from the hedgerows and meadows near the boatyard, and are in a pitcher from a fair. The simplicity of the arrangement is somehow more appropriate to a humble fishing boat than a large bunch of blooms would be.

the romantic *garden shed*

The words "romantic" and "garden shed" are not often used together. But the delightful summerhouse on these and the following two pages is just that. It was built over a period of three months for Kerstin Rodgers (whose home is featured on pages 120–127) by a carpenter friend, using wood and architectural materials that had almost completely been salvaged from scrapheaps, including those outside DIY stores, where damaged store goods are thrown away. Two of its windows—including the stained-glass window—were literally found on the street, and others came from DIY stores. Kerstin sometimes serves Underground Supper Club meals here, as it's a charming and unusual venue to find in a big city.

There is now a huge variety of garden rooms available, from chain-store self-assembly wooden sheds to sophisticated buildings with insulation, electrics, and plumbing, but the latter are expensive. Depending on where you live, how large your garden is, and what sort of a shed you're considering, you may need planning permission, but in most countries a modest garden shed is not something that planning authorities will necessarily get involved in.

You can also download advice and plans for building your own shed from the internet, although, of course, you can't necessarily tell which plans are the best. Another suggestion, if you want to save money, and don't have any carpentry or DIY skills, is to find out if there are any skill-share schemes locally, or set one up yourself. A skill-share scheme is when you exchange your skills for someone else's on an hourly basis, so you might, for example, exchange five hours of catering for five hours of carpentry.

Above right: A detail of the stained-glass window, which was rescued from the street—one of many pieces of architectural reclamation used to build the hut.

Center right: Kerstin loves poppies, and her mother stitched this tapestry throw pillow for her.

Below right: This quirky little bird house came from Florida.

Far right: The photograph was taken in the Himalayas by Kerstin, and the vintage frame was a present from friends.

Overleaf left: The interior of the summerhouse is furnished with an old French bed from the largest flea-market in the world—the Braderie de Lille, which happens on the first weekend of September in Lille, France. The low rocking chair was a present.

Overleaf right: The wood-burning stove came from an auction, and the wire baskets on the shelves were being thrown out from an open-air swimming pool, where they were used for swimmers to store their clothes in.

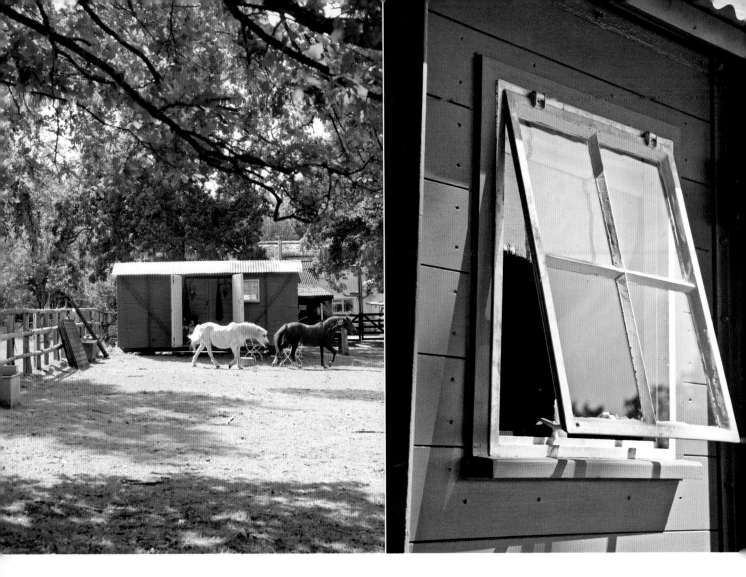

the railway *wagon*

This railway wagon belongs to photographer Ari Ashley, who bought it from an online auction for $150 (£100) because she wanted some extra storage. It arrived on a flat-bed truck and was lifted into position with a crane. She never thought of sleeping in it, but it needed some repair, and as she took it apart she began to "marvel at the quality of manufacturing at the time it was made." She cleaned off all the rust, and replaced 80 percent of the internal wood, and suddenly the wagon came to life. It's now a charming hideaway, spare bedroom, and sanctuary.

Decommissioned railway stock can be found on the internet, and many people have made wagons and carriages into vacation cottages or even homes. You can also find companies specializing in delivery on the internet. There are websites where you can register that you have an item of a certain size that needs transporting from one place to another, and companies will then compete for your business. So if you are lucky—for example, if a carrier is just seeking a load to cover the return costs of another job—transport need not be too expensive.

Ari's advice is to take a project such as this slowly, and to treat it as a hobby, "so you can be proud as you complete each stage." Replacing the wood on the inside can give you the opportunity to insulate, and you can cut windows in the side or the roof. You can easily install a wood-burning stove, too, but take the appropriate fire precautions.

Above far left: The wagon shares an idyllic paddock with Ari's horses.

Above left: The window was bought from a local glass company and installed by a local carpenter.

Above: The stump of a tree is used as a side table, beside a barbecue made from the lid of a trash can. Folding garden chairs like these are easily available from most chain stores and don't take up much space.

Above right: Both the bed and the rug were recycled from Ari's house.

Overleaf left: Although Ari replaced much of the wagon's original wood with new, some old interior planking remains. She has painted the new wood, but stripped the old, to make the most of its patina and wear. The picture over the head of the bed was painted by Ari's sister, Jennifer.

Overleaf right: The two traditional folding "director's chairs" are widely available in chain stores, and Ari bought the fleeces from a butcher in Wales. The picture of carrots was painted by Ari's husband, Nick Ashley. The storage cabinet, with its mesh door, came from a country secondhand shop.

Ari painted the interior white to maximize light and furnished the wagon very simply with a mix of flea-market finds and furniture she already had. The bed and rug came from her home, and the rest was collected over time. There's a basic theme of stripes: a striped blanket, towel, and blind. It's not "matchy-matchy," but it prevents a small interior from looking too busy by adding a sense of coherence.

There's no electricity, so they have to rely on lamps and candles. It is always important, though, to make sure that a naked candle flame can't tip over.

Left: The blanket on the bed is a piece of railway memorabilia bought on an online auction. There is a paraffin lamp on the wall, and its light is good enough to read by. The dustpan and brush came from vintage household stockists Labour and Wait, and the window shade and the striped linen came from Ari's mother's store, Diana McNair-Wilson Decorative Antiques. The blind is made from antique Hungarian linen, which Diana's mother buys from Romani travelers.
Above left: Sport-themed tankards are typical flea-market fare—they cost hardly anything and you can build up quite a collection.
Above right: The horse theme again, this time on a set of glasses—so appropriate for a wagon set down in a paddock.

shabby chic *gardens*

Above left: An old kettle makes a fun container for lavender.

Above center: Old Victorian terracotta flower pots planted up with sedums and displayed together in a wire basket. A grouping of similar plants and containers always looks good together.

Above right: A collection of vintage watering cans adds atmosphere, but they are also still in use. Old garden tools can often be found at garage or car boot sales, and they add character to a garden.

Right: This cast-iron arch was bought on the internet and gives a sense of height and proportion to the garden. eBay is often a good place to find such pieces.

The shabby chic look works particularly well in gardens, because it doesn't matter if furniture gets more weathered. You can achieve a "secret garden" effect even in the smallest of backyards with some trellis or an arch covered in climbing roses.

This look is essentially romantic, with an abundance of planting. In a city, with walls all around, gardens tend to be shady, so you need to choose plants carefully in order to get the lush look. Climbers in particular may shoot up the wall or arch and try to bloom in your neighbor's garden. 'Madame Albert Carrière', for example, is a climbing rose that thrives in shade, and there are many others.

Shade-loving plants do have flowers, but in a small garden you won't get the display you would expect in a larger space. This is where container plants— effectively flower-arranging outside—come in. Every market has its plant stall, and there'll always be a bargain, such as lavender, bulbs about to flower, or geraniums. Use cans, tins, jars, pots—or even more unusual receptacles such as kettles—to add color to your garden. The plants won't grow properly in a small container, and need drainage holes cut in the base for long-term use, but they will look fresh and fun for a month or so. After that, you can replace them with whatever's next in season.

vintage *and modern*

This tiny courtyard, surrounded by lush growth, is a charming, private green space in the heart of the city. Furnished with a mix of new garden furniture and vintage finds, it has a charming French feel to it.

You can find wrought iron furniture at every price point, and it's also gradually making its way to the secondhand market. Whether you buy new from a chain store or secondhand, make sure that chairs and tables are stable and strong enough to use. There's no need to look for matching sets as it's often cheaper to buy an odd chair or table and build up a collection. Look in the bargain area of garden stores, on the internet, or in secondhand stores.

If you stick to a theme, such as wrought iron or teak, different styles of chairs and tables will look good together. Using the same colors throughout the garden will also achieve the same effect. For example, you could use one shade of gray, white, or blue on garden gates, furniture, and even sheds. You shouldn't paint hardwoods like teak, but metal garden furniture can always be painted with either an outside paint or a specialist metal paint.

Left: Vintage garden chairs with a bench from a garden chain store. The vivid pink tablecloth adds a splash of color to a shady spot. Outside rooms are usually within easy reach of the house, so cloths and cushions can easily be taken in during bad weather, but you can also build or buy bench seating to store fabrics that can't be left outside.

Above left: The owner collects stone and stone-colored planters—more unusual than the usual terracotta and they all work well together.

Above right: The table, without its cloth, can be seen from the windows of the house, so it provides the perfect display place for these planters, which are ablaze with bulbs.

a pretty *pergola*

The garden as an outside room is a major direction these days. Even if you have only a small terrace, you can increase your living space in summer months. If you don't have the money—or can't get the planning permission—to build a gazebo or summerhouse, a simple frame pergola, planted with vines and strung with fairy lights, makes a delightful place to sit out. Most gardens benefit from the sense of height these give, too, as they often improve the proportions. And, of course, they help with privacy and shade. A pergola is not just a structure to train plants up, it is also a frame for a seating area.

You can sometimes buy whole pergolas, usually iron ones, at salvage yards, but otherwise stout timbers or posts can often be acquired cheaply. These should be sunk well into the ground to give them support, and then secured by several overhead timbers across the top.

Having created a roof, you can hang a chandelier. You may find chandeliers that have been wired up for electricity, but it's relatively simple to remove these fittings to use candles again, and if the chandelier is metal, it can then go outside. Never wire up electrical chandeliers for outdoor use unless you've had specialist advice.

Above left: Glass and mesh food domes are experiencing a revival at the moment. With the advent of refrigerators to the mass market in the 1950s and then commercial plastic wrap in the 1960s, domes were discarded as old fashioned. However, domes are perfect for storing food at room temperature while offering protection from flies, without the chemicals of plastic wrap. Food domes are now available in chain stores, or you can look out for them in flea markets.

Above center: This large circular metal tray was bought from an online auction. It works very well as a lazy Susan in the center of the table.

Above right: The iron chandelier holds real candles. Always be careful that the flames will not reach the timbers or any climbing plants that are dangling down.

Right: The chairs and tables are a mix of old and new and have been collected over the years. The large table is made up of two inexpensive standard tables pushed together. The throw pillows are made from Swedish grain sacks.

Fleamarkets

Check tourist and town information services for details of regular markets and car boot fairs.

United States

The world's largest yard sale is a four-day sale which starts on the first Thursday in August, and stretches 675 miles (1,087 km), going through five states from Hudson, Michigan to Gadsden, Alabama. See www.127sale.com.

Competing with it as "the world's largest garage sale" is the Warrensburg Garage Sale held in Warrensburg, NY, on the first weekend in October—see www.warrensburggaragesale.com.

Rose Bowl Flea Market at UCLA Bruins Football Stadium in Pasadena, California, takes place on the second Sunday of each month. See www.rgcshows.com for this and other markets.

Hell's Kitchen Flea Market New York is held on West 39th Street between 9th and 10th Avenues, with secondhand designer clothing and vintage household wares. See www.hellskitchenfleamarket.com.

United Kingdom

In Britain, you can find local car boot fairs on www.carbootjunction.com/www.carbootsales.org.

There is a "flea market" element to most big antiques trade sales—these start early in the morning and are usually over by lunchtime. Find out more about the International Antique and Collectors Fair (held at Newark, Ardingly, Shepton Mallet, Newbury, Swinderby, Redbourn, and North Weald) at www.iacf.co.uk. Also take a look at the top antiques trade market at Kempton Park, Surrey—see www.kemptonantiques.com.

The New Caledonian Market (Bermondsey Market) is open every Friday morning, 5am–9am, in Bermondsey Square, London SE1 4QB.

Canada

Toronto's largest indoor flea market is Dr Flea's www.drfleas.com. For Ontario flea markets, consult www.ontariofleamarkets.com.

Australia

There's a guide to Sydney's markets on www.sydney.world-guides.com, including flea markets and antiques markets. Melbourne's flea markets can be found on www.whitehat.com.au.

Europe

Paris's largest flea market is a collection of 15 markets based near Porte de Clignancourt, Paris, Saturday—Monday. See www.parispuces.com.

La Braderie in Lille, France, is Europe's largest flea market and is a two-day event in September. See www.lilletourism.com.

Look out for "warehouse markets," especially the Mercatino di Torino in Turin, Italy (see www.mercatinotorino.altervista.org), where second-hand goods are sold on behalf of their owners. Addresses can be found in tourist centers.

Asia

Seasoned travelers particularly recommend the Panjiayuan Flea Market in Beijing, China.

Resources

Achillea Flowers (pages 126–127)
92 Mill Lane, London NW6 1NL
020 7431 1727 www.achilleaflowers.com
Beautiful flowers and unusual old containers.

Ashley Stores (pages 146–151)
57 Ledbury Road, London W11 2AA

John Bennett Fine Paintings (page 37)
020 8748 1747
www.johnbennettfinepaintings.co.uk

Julia Dickens (page 68)
Water color artist
Hindhead, Surrey, 01428 605729

Lucy Dickens (pages 74–85)
www.lucydickens.com

Zita Elze (pages 106–115)
Designer florist
287 Sandycombe Road, Kew, Richmond, Surrey TW9 3LU www.zitaelze.com

Foxed Grey (pages 106–115)
Antique and vintage furniture
25 West St, Chichester, West Sussex PO19 1RZ
02392 413619 www.foxedgrey.com

Helena Gavshon Design for Textiles (pages 34–37 and 56–67)
6 South Street, London W10 5PH
0208 969 7280 www.helenagavshon.com

Mark Hearld (pages 128–133)
Illustrator and artist Contact via mark.a.hearld@googlemail.com
Printed textiles designed by Mark Hearld are available from www.stjudesfabrics.co.uk

i gigi General Store (pages 86–105)
31A Weston Road, Hove, East Sussex BN3 1AF
01273 775257 www.igigigeneralstore.com

Celia Lewis (pages 44 and 46)
Artist www.celialewis.co.uk

Diana McNair-Wilson Decorative Antiques
0207 937 3564

Melanie Molesworth (pages 106–117)
Interior stylist
The Arched House, Lyme Regis
07976 721429
www.melaniemolesworthstylist.co.uk

Old Albion Antiques (pages 106–115)
Furniture and vintage interiors
54D St Michael's, Bridport, Dorset, DT6 3RR
0787 905 1362 www.oldalbion.co.uk

Kerstin Rodgers (pages 120–127 and 142–145)
The Underground Restaurant
www.marmitelover.blogspot.com
The Underground Restaurant can be booked via www.wegottickets.com/undergroundrestaurant.

Henny Tate (pages 44–55)
Interior designer
Oak House Studio , West Street, Aldbourne Wiltshire SN8 2BS
01672 541762 www.hennytate.com

Rutledge Turnlund
Contact via rutledge.turnlund@gmail.com

Index

Acknowledgments

A huge thank you to Simon Brown for the wonderful photographs, which capture the essence of all the lovely homes, and to all the flea-market aficionados who generously let us photograph them. They include Ari Ashley, Lucy Dickens, Zoe Ellison, Helena Gavshon, Mark Hearld, Alex Logendre, Melanie Molesworth, Alex and Sophie Smith, Henny Tate, Kerstin Rodgers, Rutledge Turnlund, Posy Gentles, and Kim Ward, who shared their top tips.

Thank you to the team at CICO Books: Cindy Richards, Gillian Haslam, Sally Powell, and Carmel Edmonds, and especially the designer, Louise Leffler.